W9-DEO-744

Teaching Children
To Read Music

Teaching Children To Read Music

CHARLES W. HEFFERNAN
Arizona State University

Appleton-Century-Crofts
Division of Meredith Corporation / New York

MIT
236
.H 54

688-1

Library of Congress Card Number: 68-55077

PRINTED IN THE UNITED STATES OF AMERICA
E43073

Preface

During the twenty-odd years that I have been conducting church choirs and community, high school, and college choruses, my attention has been frequently drawn to the singers' inability to read music, to understand the printed page of music symbols. In spite of six or eight years of music instruction in public schools, these enthusiastic music lovers rarely demonstrate a knowledge of music fundamentals which exceeds the level of insignificance.

Music reading is often neglected in elementary school music classes. It is more immediately satisfying to have children learn songs by rote; teaching the rudiments is likely to be dismissed as dull, uncreative, and out-of-date. This is a regrettable situation because some schools have shown that it *is* possible to teach children to read music fluently, that their ability to read immeasurably increases their comprehension and enjoyment of music, and that learning to read music need not be a dull, joyless, and uncreative experience.

The ability to read music must be gained over a long, carefully planned period of development. There are no shortcuts or tricks that enable a person to acquire the skill overnight. The time to begin is when the child is in the elementary school.

Many years of thought and teaching have preceded the writing of this book. I am forever indebted to three different groups which helped to solidify the concepts presented here: (1) the boys and girls in the public schools of Fryeburg, Maine, and Conway, New Hampshire, who were such a stimulus to me as a young teacher and who became a proving ground for my philosophy of music education; (2) my professors and good friends at The University of Michigan who inspired me to codify my thoughts on the subject of music reading; and (3) my pupils in music education classes at the University of Washington and Oakland University who, in embarking on careers in elementary music teaching, convinced me of the need for this book.

C. W. H.

v

Contents

Preface   v

Introduction   1
1. The Problem Defined   4
2. The Readiness Program   9
3. Reading Rhythm   24
4. Reading Pitch   40
5. Reading Dynamic Indications   58
6. Independent Music Reading   64

   Appendix A.   The Music-Reading Continuum   89
   Appendix B.   Music-Reading Activities by
                   Grade Level   95

Bibliography   97

Introduction

SINCE THE DAYS of Guido d'Arezzo, inventor of the staff and teacher of young musicians, music educators have been greatly concerned with the difficulties of teaching people to read music. Indeed, it is doubtful if all the other aspects of music teaching have together received the attention and thought that have been lavished upon the methodology involved in translating music symbols into the patterns of sound they represent.

In the United States, music education had its beginning in the eighteenth century, when singing schools flourished in the colonies. The primary purpose of the singing schools was to teach people to read music. Lowell Mason, who began to teach music in the Boston schools in 1837, was a singing master, and his public school music classes differed little from his work in the singing schools.

From Lowell Mason's time until well into the twentieth century, the public school music curriculum was almost entirely devoted to music reading. Pedagogues and publishers pooled their efforts and came up with an astonishing array of methodological devices, many of which are only today being rediscovered. The school music books of the late nineteenth century abound in teaching aids such as staffs which are gradually expanded from a single line to the customary five lines, charts to teach the syllables for pitch

1

reading, modulators to explain simple key changes, tables of time-names and rhythm patterns, and hundreds of inane little tunes upon which the children were to practice their reading skills.

By about 1920, the music curriculum had expanded to include rhythmic activities, music appreciation, and the study of instruments. Within a few years, today's six-fold program was well established: singing, rhythms, reading, listening, instrumental music, and some attention to creative activities and music in drama. In the face of this expanded program, music reading was either exalted or neglected according to the particular interests of the authors and publishers of the period.

The most recent school music publications illustrate this situation. In some books the concentration on developing singing voices, playing instruments, and expressing music through play or dance practically excludes mention of the elements of notation and development of reading ability, which apparently the children are supposed to obtain by some sort of osmosis. Such books are often thought to be forward looking or progressive in their concept. Other school music books build their program around a repertoire of songs especially composed to teach the fundamental steps in music reading. These books, however, rarely proceed beyond the most elementary stages of notation, and they provide almost no exposure to legitimate music.

Books on the teaching of music in schools all contain some mention of the desirability of teaching children to read music. But, once the topic has been introduced, the degree to which it is developed is determined largely by the author's interest in the subject, which—in recent publications—ranges from minimal to considerable. This divergence of viewpoint is perpetuated in college teacher-training classes and is taken by young music teachers into the schools, where music reading may or may not receive adequate attention.

There are at least two reasons for a renewal of interest in teaching music reading in public school classes. First, an emphasis on music reading would do much to stabilize the enigmatical course of our present elementary school music curriculum. Music in the elementary schools of the United States is suffering dreadfully from a lack of direction; the multiplicity of activities carried on in the name of music classes for children is completely out of hand. Music teachers often pride themselves on the lengths to which a song may be stretched—clapping the beat while singing, learning a descant, adding instruments, creating additional verses, making up a dance, capturing the mood of the song in finger paints, dramatizing the story of the song, visiting the violin-maker's shop, doing research on the country from whence the song came, and viewing slides of the teacher's recent trip to Java. Some of these activities are unquestionably valuable, but too many classes never seem to progress beyond such a state of nervous activity. So little measurable learning takes place in this feverish atmosphere that one might wonder if music is the one subject in elementary school that can be taught with the same methods, materials, and objectives in grade six as in grade one. If music is to continue as an important part of the school curriculum, it must become a subject that is studied diligently and in a dignified manner; as in other subjects, there should be a logical progression of studies and some objective evaluation of the learning which has taken place. An emphasis on music reading would do much to accomplish these aims.

A second reason for teaching music reading may be found in an examination of the current state of our home and community amateur music making. Somehow, active participation in music must become more widespread. Our secondary schools should have singing assemblies as well as gatherings to listen to the selected *a cappella* chorus; churches should have vigorous congregational singing in addition to fine anthems by the choir; in addition to supporting the urban professional orchestras, our communities and suburbs should abound with amateur choral and chamber music societies. These developments cannot take place until our populace has, as part of its general education, the ability to translate printed music symbols into sound. This ability, even in moderate degree, permits one to study, perform, and hence to understand better much of our vast heritage of music, one of our most important expressions of artistic endeavor.

Chapter 1
The Problem
Defined

THE ABILITY to read music, to change the page of printed music notation into sound, is a skill which is gradually acquired. Some people seem to grasp the idea easily while others, even after years of music study, are extremely poor readers. Music teachers are in no way united on the answer to the question of what constitutes a successful music-reading program in school. Many teachers are satisfied if their classes, as a whole, can sing a simple melody while it is played on the piano. Others drill at length on syllables or numbers while many care not a whit for any aspect of the problem.

There is considerable confusion in the very term *music reading*. In seeking a definition, let us consider several situations:

(1) A child of about seven years is asked to examine a rhythmic pattern placed on the blackboard— ♩ ♩ ♫ ♩. After he looks at it for a moment, the teacher asks him to chant it aloud. The child responds, "walk, walk, run-run, walk" in precisely the rhythm notated. The teacher hands him a small drum and a beater. He then

plays the pattern in the rhythm he has just chanted. Can we say that this child reads music?

(2) The conductor of a noted college choir has taken his group to a new auditorium for a rehearsal. The choir is arranged, and the accompanist takes his place at the organ console. The conductor gives the downbeat and the first notes of Bach's *Jesu Meine Freude* peal forth. However, after about two chords, the conductor claps his hands over his ears and shouts, "The organ is two cycles *sharp!*" It was later ascertained that the instrument was *exactly* two cycles sharp—its A sounded 442 vibrations per second. This conductor has an excellent ear. Is he necessarily a good reader?

(3) Jim Smith has been a member of his church choir for several years. He has a pleasing bass voice which serves as a model for the other basses. Indeed, whenever Jim is absent, the quality of the bass section is noticeably poorer. At a rehearsal one evening, the choir was reading through several new anthems. Things were not going too well. Finally the director asked in desperation, "What is the matter with the basses?" Somewhat uncomfortably, Jim replied, "Charlie's not here," naming a quiet, unobtrusive gentleman who always sat beside him. Charlie can read music and actually teaches the part to Jim, who learns it rapidly and accurately. But, what is the level of Jim Smith's music-reading ability?

(4) A colleague of mine at the University of Washington plays the piano fluently. People watch in amazement as he sits and plays from a full orchestral score, reducing many lines of music for various transposing instruments in several clefs. He plays with expression, commenting on the construction of the work, unusual harmonic progressions, or hidden contrapuntal devices. We can safely say that he reads music.

We might, of course, continue with many more situations of this nature, such as prima donnas who learn their roles only with the diligent patience of a note-driller or the college piano major who plays Rachmaninoff concertos but cannot read at sight the simplest accompaniment to a solo. However, further elaboration should not be necessary, for the point to be made here is that while each case mentioned involves a person who reads music to *some* extent, the *range* of abilities covered by the term *music-reading skill* is tremendous. Of the people just mentioned, two may be said to represent the limits of this range. At the bottom of the scale would be the child who, with no hint of rote assistance, chants or plays a rhythm pattern containing notes of two different time values. Simple as the problem appears, the child is definitely reading music. At the top of the scale is my colleague at the University who, while looking at the score, solves a multitude of rhythmic, pitch, and interpretive directions simultaneously and with such ease that his playing seems to be directed subconsciously.

Between these two extremes we could arbitrarily place the other people we have mentioned. Most of them would cluster near the bottom of the scale. However, the choral conductor with the acute sense of pitch would probably be well toward the top, and the quiet Charlie in the church choir would be somewhere near the middle.

Extremes of Music-Reading Skill

First page of Brahms' First Symphony reproduced by permission of Breitkopf & Härtel, Wiesbaden.

The music-reading *continuum,* the term used to describe the range of reading skills, is long and complex. A multitude of learning experiences takes place along it, and many years of study are required before one completes the journey from start to finish.

As we consider this continuum, two familiar principles of teaching should be obvious. First, it is apparent that music-reading ability at any point on the scale is dependent upon an amalgamation of the learning experiences previously encountered. There are four simple problems to be solved while reading music—*when* to play the note, *how long* to sustain it, *what* note to play, and *how* to play it. At any point on the continuum there must be an immediate and correct solution to these four problems if reading is to take place. A reader returns constantly to problems encountered separately at a lower level on the continuum. For example, a person playing from a full orchestral score will very likely be called upon to solve a rhythmic pattern similar to the one the child played near the beginning of the continuum—♩ ♩ ♫ ♩. Although the notes may be played on different pitches and with dynamic contrasts, the basic problem of ♩ ♩ ♫ ♩ remains.

Secondly, any new experience on the continuum must be logically associated with the learning which has immediately preceded it. For example, suppose the first lessons on the continuum are confined only to reading rhythms. After the class gains some facility, the teacher introduces the concept of pitch without reference to reading rhythm. It is very likely that the studies in reading pitch will never really congeal and, unless somehow attached to the previous main body of acquired knowledge, will probably wither away. The teacher becomes discouraged with the results of his teaching and gives up the whole plan to teach his class to read.

These two items, which together are really nothing more than carefully planned continuity, are the key to a successful program of music reading in elementary school. Yet, however simple and apparent the problem seems to be, teachers are likely to wander aimlessly up and down the continuum with no plan in mind and with only a faint hope of their classes learning to read.

To teach music reading successfully, a teacher must be able to view the continuum as a whole, evaluate the present capabilities of the students, and proceed from that point on the continuum where the evaluation places the student. Hit-or-miss flings at clapping rhythms, singing tonal patterns, learning the key signature for E major, and making Indian drums in music class will not produce music readers.

It should be possible to proceed along the continuum slowly and steadily from the time the child enters school. At the end of the sixth grade, he will not be playing from full orchestral scores, but he may have a foundation that permits him to do so at a later time. At the end of the sixth grade, a child should be able to sing at sight a diatonic melody whose range does not exceed a twelfth and whose rhythmic complexities are not great. He should be able to play these melodies on the piano or on bells. He should understand the concept of key and know the most common tempo and dynamic indications. These abilities constitute what might be considered a reasonable ability in music reading for children in the sixth grade.

SUGGESTIONS FOR FURTHER STUDY

The following readings, drawn from prominent publications on elementary school music, are selective in nature rather than general or all-inclusive. For the most part, they reiterate viewpoints and procedures explained in the preceding chapter; in some cases, the reading presents a conflicting opinion.

GARRETSON, Robert L. *Music in Childhood Education.* New York: Appleton-Century-Crofts, 1966. Pages 163-164.

NYE, Robert E., and NYE, Vernice T. *Music in the Elementary School,* 2nd ed. Englewood Cliffs, N. J.: Prentice-Hall, 1964. Pages 296-303.

Chapter 2

The Readiness Program

BEFORE ANY ATTEMPT is made to familiarize the child with the intricacies of printed music notation, it is absolutely essential that he experience a wide variety of musical activities. It is preposterous to expect a child to be interested in solving the printed score unless he has participated in and enjoyed many aspects of music. Programs of music reading are often begun too early, before the child has gained a sufficient variety and depth of musical experience.

Many parallels may be drawn between the teaching of the reading of words and the reading of music, and the music teacher would do well to review his knowledge of the development of language-reading ability. The young child learns to call objects by name by imitating his parents, his older brothers and sisters, or other adults. Gradually, he learns to combine words into phrases or sentences, and, as he matures, his vocabulary expands. He is able to converse with considerable ease at a fairly early age, well before he tries to read printed words.

At some point, he discovers books, which are, of course, merely playthings. He soon learns, however, to turn the pages and enjoy the pictures. He likes to have his parents read to him, and gradually he comes to recognize which book contains his favorite story. Some children are remarkably quick at associating single printed words with the object they symbolize; by three or four years of age, many children can follow along the sentences which are being read to them. They may not recognize many words, but they are developing eye movement from left to right and are associating printed symbols with sound. What parent has not tried to hurry through the evening reading by omitting some phrases only to have his child point out with indignation, "You left *that* out!"

When the time comes for the child to enter school, he probably has considerable ability with spoken words. He may not be able to interpret any printed symbols, but he is at least familiar with books and printing. He is observed by his teacher and, when the time seems appropriate, embarks on the particular reading program in vogue at the time and, hopefully, learns to read. It may be a long time before he reads with comprehension; he may never read with dramatic expression; years will pass before he can unlock the majesty of a Shakespearean soliloquy.

The child's preschool music experience is likely to be considerably less than his acquaintance with language. Many children have musical toys from an early age, thereby providing the ear with varieties of sound. Mothers (and fathers also, for that matter) may sing to their babies, and children may in infancy coo softly, which is an elementary stage of vocal production. Children today are, of course, exposed to a great deal of music on the radio, television, and recordings. The side of their musical development which is most likely to be passed by is their active participation. Merely bathing in organized sound, strangely enough, does not seem to develop appreciably the urge to perform. The desire to sing, play instruments, dance, and create melodies arises from associating with others who do these things. Unless the child is raised in a musically active home, he will arrive in the kindergarten or first grade with a very low musical experience level.

The primary grades teacher is therefore faced with the problem of raising the child's musical experience level by means of activities which correspond roughly with those events of preschool years that provide the basis for speaking and language teaching. Music teachers and primary classroom teachers undoubtedly err in trying to interest the children in music which is much too complicated. Catchy, pseudo-commercial popular songs with tricky accompaniments should be removed from the primary grades. There should be more emphasis on experimenting with sound, the raw material from which music is made. Observe the two-year-old beating tirelessly on a drum, box, or kitchen utensil or the somewhat older child improvising a rhythmic chant using only two notes that are a minor third apart. They are fulfilling a need for personal expression. If this need is blocked by the teacher's insistence that Jimmy play on the unaccented beats, alternating with the teacher's accented ones, the first cracks in the music-reading continuum may be created right at the very foundation.

Let us now discuss in detail the musical experiences which might be carried out by the primary grades teacher before an attempt is made at reading music notation. Some of these activities may have been taken care of during the preschool years. It is, therefore, the teacher's task to evaluate constantly the experience level of his class and to try to lay a broad, firm foundation of musical learning upon which progress may be solidly built.

First, the child must be encouraged to participate actively in the performance of music. The teacher must begin with songs of a very simple nature, which he shares with the children, encouraging them to sing with him. Much thought must be given to the selection of these songs. They should be limited in range (a fifth or sixth is sufficient) and very simple rhythmically. They must be thoroughly learned by the teacher and presented to the children with joy, conviction, and naturalness, together with precise diction and excellent musicianship. The key should be carefully selected so that the children are not forced into uncomfortable ranges; the octave between middle C and C above is best for children in the early primary grades. Needless to say, the teacher must be free from his books.

There is an extreme unevenness of musical value in the many books of children's songs published today. Hundreds of inane, tiresome tunes, composed for a price by musically illiterate pedagogues, daily stifle musical development in our schools. The teacher must rely on his own musical judgment to discern and cast out these monstrosities. There is no lack of beautiful songs for children to sing; one must, however, search for them. The children themselves will help separate the wheat from the chaff.

The question of suitable accompaniment for children's singing has received considerable discussion in recent publications. Some teachers like to sit at the piano, playing the melody very quietly with a simple chordal accompaniment. The tastefully played guitar and autoharp are also quite effective. The accompaniment should enhance the song and never detract from it. The key of the song should be changed frequently for the sake of interest and so that the range of the children's voices may be extended.

The repertoire of the class should grow steadily, and a variety of tempos, moods, modes, and meters should be planned. In addition to those songs which the class sings, the teacher alone should sing other songs for the children's pleasure, perhaps inviting them to join in only at certain reiterated phrases or at the refrain.

Once the singing activity is well established, children should be encouraged to accompany the singing of the class on simple instruments. Drums of various sizes, wood blocks, rattles, sticks, and triangles should be available in order that the children may choose the appropriate timbre for a certain song. Given a choice of chords on the autoharp, a child will quickly learn to select tonic or dominant at the right time to fit the turn of the melody. Bells, tone-bars, and other percussion instruments of definite pitch will help the child to listen more acutely. Ear training, or discriminatory listening, is generally neglected in the elementary school, and it should be started as early as possible.

Again, the playing of instruments should enhance the singing. The player must listen carefully so that he may play at the appropriate time, which is likely to be on every beat. Different instruments may occasionally play together. The overall sound should not be too complex, and the emphasis should lie on discriminating listening in an atmosphere of spontaneity, always under the evaluative eye and ear of the teacher.

Great emphasis should be placed on creativity in children's musical activity. In these early stages of musical experience building, it is essential that every child be encouraged to create his own text to simple tunes, to construct his own little melodies, and to present his own interpretations. To promote creativity in his music classes, the teacher might sing:

I   see   a   tree.

and encourage the children, one at a time, to sing to the class what he sees in the room or outside the window. Let the enthusiastic ones begin, but always try to draw out the less exuberant. Give praise liberally!

Soon the children will be able to improvise their texts and melodies simultaneously, and the rest of the class can learn Becky's or Billy's song about coming to school, climbing a tree, or riding on the bus. A teacher with a good ear can easily construct simple accompaniments to these child creations and so enhance them greatly. When a child of six hears his peers singing *his* song, the look in his eyes and on his face will tell the teacher that he has awakened the child's mind and so made possible further learning.

Admittedly, this creative atmosphere is difficult to generate and maintain. Young music teachers are notably uncreative. Whatever creativity they may have possessed in childhood has often been slowly beaten out of them during years of practicing, completing theory exercises, and performing in dictator-managed ensembles. Teachers who have struggled for years to learn cycles of German lieder may have trouble improvising a three-tone song or in becoming enthusiastic over simple songs constructed by their classes. The intelligent teacher, however, needs only to see each activity in its proper place on the music-reading continuum and realize the many steps that must be traversed before the children reach his level of musical experience.

The second area of music-reading readiness which should be prepared is that of rhythms. The children, of course, have been experiencing rhythmic patterns in their songs and have been playing simple instruments while singing, but there are several other kinds of rhythmic activities which will do much to help the child feel secure in reading rhythmic notation.

The teacher and his class might experiment with three forms of locomotor movement—walking, running, and skipping. The class members should perform these movements as the teacher weaves them into a story, play, or other creative endeavor. The walking, running, and skipping movement of the children should be accompanied by a drum or other percussion instrument with appropriate rhythms— ♩ ♩ ♩ ♩ for walking, ♫ ♫ ♫ ♫ for running, and ♪. ♪. ♪. ♪. for skipping. The physical movement and the appropriate *aural* rhythmic pattern must be thoroughly coordinated in the child's musical consciousness by means of three steps: (1) *responding* with the correct movement to the appropriate drum pattern; (2) *substituting* a *spoken* rhythm pattern of walk-walk-walk-walk or run-run-run-run, or skipty-skipty-skipty-skipty in place of the physical movement when the drum pattern is heard; and (3) *playing* on a drum or other instrument the correct pattern for walking, running, or skipping as requested by the teacher or other children. The children should eventually be able on request to respond in motion, speak in rhythm, or play on a drum the three basic rhythms. They should be able to do any one, two, or even all three activities simultaneously (marching, chanting walk-walk-walk-walk, and playing quarter notes on the drum).

Since the study of rhythms permeates all musical learning, it is worthy of isolation and study in its simplest forms. Although rhythm is often taught as such, it is not a mental concept, but rather motion and physical response. It should be studied from this standpoint. One of the greatest mistakes in teaching music is to begin with the whole note, *explaining* that it has four beats and that it can be divided and played with one-beat notes, two-beat notes, or even two notes to one beat. It is remarkable that children subjected to such methods ever learn to read music fluently. Of course, few do.

The quarter note is the basis of our system of music notation, and every effort should be made to teach people how to produce a flow of quarter notes with absolute regularity. One of the best ways this may be accomplished is by correlating quarter notes with the physical motion of walking, which most children and adults do with perfect evenness. Running produces eighth notes, and skipping is done in a rhythm which approximates a dotted eighth followed by a sixteenth note. Therefore, by utilizing three basic rhythms, three of the most important patterns of conventional music notation can be experienced aurally at an early age.

Rhythmic activities in the early grades should also include the introduction of the concept of extended patterns of sound, which we may call *phrases.* For example, the teacher might demonstrate the simple act of stretching. After the children have tried it a few times the teacher could play appropriate music on the piano:

Stretch up!   Hold!   Relax!

After a few tries, the teacher can augment this basic pattern in many ways, such as extending the length of the stretch with additional chords; holding, trilling, or otherwise ornamenting the *fermata;* and varying the speed and intensity of the relax phrase. Children love surprises, and they will quickly learn to follow the teacher's variations on this pattern, which can be infinite. The teacher should try to develop *active, perceptive* listening.

It is a simple step from response with axial movement to perceptive listening to phrases that can be expressed in locomotor movement. For example, the children might be asked to respond to music such as:

Two contrasting movements are about all the children can be expected to handle. The phrases should be kept short and should be repeated to form periods of four or eight measures. The students are thus presented with the idea of repetition. More subtle variations on this activity might include marching in circles or straight lines with a change of direction when the music suggests it. The teacher may play these phrases on a drum:

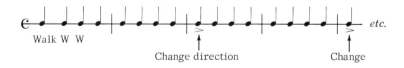

For these creative rhythmic activities, the ability to improvise at the piano can be most helpful, and all teachers should try to develop freedom at the keyboard. Playing only on the black keys is a good way to start. From there, facility in many keys is more easily obtained. The use of rather abrupt key changes will point up more clearly the phrases.

Pooh's March

Action songs and singing games can play an important part in developing attention to musical phrases. "I'm a Little Teapot," "Eency, Weency Spider," "Looby Loo," and other songs with axial and locomotor movement are always enjoyed by children. The appropriate action or movement is usually motivated by a significant word—"I put my right hand *in*."

A successful variation of this game consists of playing the music of a familiar action song and asking the children not to sing, but rather to do only the actions at the time indicated by the music. Children have great fun doing this and especially enjoy it when the teacher alters the tempo or holds back an important chord which is the signal for a certain movement. Young teachers may not, for some time, fully appreciate the attentive listening habits which children will cultivate as they enjoy this simple activity. It is highly recommended as a useful step in the development of perceptive listening.

By about the time the children have reached the end of the first grade or perhaps during the early weeks of grade two, they should be ready to do some rhythmic movement to more involved music. For teaching response to beat and turn of phrase, the music of many of our traditional folk dances is most adaptable. There are many excellent recordings of folk-dance music available today. The best ones are played by simple combinations of instruments and are free from calls and singing.

This is not to advocate the teaching of complicated dance routines to first graders. It can, of course, be done, but six-year-olds dancing the Virginia Reel smacks of exploitation. It is rather a suggestion that simple patterns of childhood movement be constructed by the teacher and the children and fitted to tunes which, as a rule, lend themselves very well to such activity.

For example, here is a simple dance which was worked out with a group of first graders to the traditional English folk dance "Greensleeves."

Formation: Double circle, partners hold inside hands, other hand propped up on hip. Couples are numbered alternately *one* and *two*.

Moderato · Greensleeves · Arr. C.W.H.

Measures 1–8: Children march in a circle for sixteen steps, swinging inside hands.

Repeat of measures 1–8: *Ones* drop hands, turn around to face *twos*, join hands all around to make little circles of four people. Turn circles once around to the left, then back to the right. (Four measures for each direction.)

Measures 9–16: All clap hands four times in front, four times over head, four times behind back, four times in front. Repeat from beginning as many times as desired.

In constructing such little dances, one must remember that perceptive listening with active response is the aim. The movement patterns, therefore, should be simple and easily learned so that the children can concentrate on the music. Needless to say, the teacher does not call out what to do next. The children must listen to the music for their directions.

The third and final aspect of the reading-readiness program consists of the developing of the child's familiarity with the printed page of music. As children enjoy books of stories and pictures, so do they love song books, and teachers in primary grades should be sure that attractive books of songs are around the room for the children's perusal. The concern at this point is only with the general impression of music symbols, not particulars or details. Children may ask as they look at music, "What is this?" "What is that mark?" "How come there are five lines?" The teacher asked these questions should first be thankful that the children are inquisitive and then tell them the legitimate name of the symbol. It is rarely necessary to give long, detailed explanations of notational details.

The blackboard can be used to good advantage during the entire reading program. In the readiness stages, the teacher should place tone-calls, phrases of the children's creation, and entire short songs in large notation on the blackboard. Other fragments of music notation may be written on illustration board and placed about the room. The teacher and the children can then sing the songs or phrases while the teacher follows the notation with his hand. This activity provides the first correlation between the rise in notation symbols and the rise in pitch, as well as the movement of music symbols from left to right. The children may like to follow

the notation with their hands themselves and should be given opportunity to do so.

There should be frequent observation of familiar songs in notation, and it is a very worthwhile activity to teach the children to
recognize familiar songs by observing the music notation only, without words. One primary music teacher has evolved a simple music
game as follows: On an easel near the piano the teacher had arranged several large cards (about 2 ft. × 3 ft). On one side of the
card would be printed a short tone-call, a phrase of music, or perhaps an entire short song. No words on this side, only music. The
teacher would then play on the piano the music from one of the
cards (which would be buried somewhere in the stack). A child
who expressed eagerness to do so would then be invited to come
forward, search through the pile for the tune that had been played,
place it on the top of the stack facing the class, and turn over the
card where the complete song with title and words would be found.
If the class found that he had chosen correctly, all would sing the
song while the child followed the notation with his hand. A simple
game, but it stimulated much interest in music notation.

Occasionally, new songs should be presented in notation while
the teacher sings the song. The technique of *watching* the general
contours of the notation at the same time one *hears* the music is
called reading music by *observation*. It is the way most musicians,
professionals and amateurs alike, read vocal music. It is a vital link
in our music-reading continuum and must receive constant,
thoughtful attention. The teacher may play through a song, asking
the children to follow along in their book or on the chart. Then he
may play it a second time and stop rather frequently, asking the
children to show him how far he has played. Then the class may
attempt to sing the entire song together. The songs selected for
observation singing should be simple, for there must be a considerable degree of success. Frequent reading of songs by observation at
all stages of the music-reading continuum is necessary for bringing
together the details of music-reading skill.

The music-reading readiness program discussed in this chapter requires about two years to accomplish. In a school system which has some sort of pre-first-grade classes (sub-primary, kindergarten, etc.), the next aspect of the reading program may be started soon after the Christmas vacation of the second grade. Sometimes, however, the readiness program is not sufficiently developed until later; it all depends on the time available for music study, the ability of the class, and the skill of the teacher in perceiving the weak spots in the children's musical development.

It is vital, as progress is made along the music-reading continuum, to restudy constantly the steps previously covered. The activities of the readiness program must be ever extended upward into the intermediate grades and beyond. Rote songs, rhythm instruments, folk games or dances, and creative music should be as important to the sixth grade as to the first.

SUMMARY

Experiences which prepare for music reading:

1. Singing many beautiful songs.
2. Creating simple melodies and rhythmic patterns.
3. Playing simple rhythm and pitch instruments.
4. Listening to music and discovering.
    A. Fast and slow
    B. Loud and soft
5. Participating in rhythmic activities.
    A. Responding to walking, running, and skipping music
    B. Experiencing phrases in dances
6. Discovering repetition in music.
    A. Melodic
    B. Rhythmic
7. Observing the printed page.

A. Horizontal and vertical aspects of notation

B. Recognizing familiar songs in notation

C. Learning new songs by observation

SUGGESTIONS FOR FURTHER STUDY

DOLL, Edna, and NELSON, Mary Jarman. *Rhythms Today!* Morristown, N. J.: Silver Burdette Company, 1965. Chapters 1 and 2.

GARRETSON, Robert L. *Music in Childhood Education.* New York: Appleton-Century-Crofts, 1966. Pages 14–31, 164–171.

NORDHOLM, Harriet. *Singing in the Elementary Schools.* Englewood Cliffs, N. J.: Prentice-Hall, 1966. Pages 3–13.

RUNKLE, Aleta, and ERICKSEN, Mary LeBow. *Music for Today's Boys and Girls.* Boston: Allyn and Bacon, 1966. Pages 33–34.

SWANSON, Bessie. *Music in the Education of Children,* 2nd ed. Belmont, Cal.: Wadsworth, 1964. Pages 17–21, 43–60, 143–170.

TIMMERMAN, Maurine. *Let's Teach Music in the Elementary School.* Evanston, Ill.: Summy-Birchard, 1958. Pages 91–96.

Chapter 3
Reading
Rhythm

AS PREVIOUSLY STATED, successful reading of music notation consists of an immediate and precise solution of four basic problems—*when* to play or sing, *how long* to sustain, *what* to play or sing, and *how*. We shall consider these problems in that order by discussing, in this chapter and the following two chapters, the reading of rhythm, pitch, and dynamics.

Probably most musicians would agree that a high percentage of the problems that a chorus or orchestra encounters in reading music are those of a rhythmic nature—the inability to maintain an appropriate tempo, the wavering of the beat, or making a mistake in the rhythmic patterns. The root of all these problems may be traced to a basic error in the teaching of music reading—the attempt to understand rhythm from the intellectual or mathematical standpoint rather than through physical motion. In view of the prevalence of these rhythmic problems, it is curious that so much music reading is taught, both vocally and instrumentally, by first considering the various *pitches* to be produced. If the notes are produced at the correct moment and sustained for their proper duration, the mere observing of the contour of the melody will many times guide the reader to the right pitch. A chorus or instrumental ensemble which is rhythmically secure can, in spite of wrong pitches, play through a composition and secure a general idea of the work. How often one hears a choral director fussing with the intonation of the first chord of a chorale only to have his labors wasted at the second beat where one part must move in a rhythm different from that of the others.

Because rhythm can be expressed with tangible, physical movement, it is actually much easier to teach than pitch, which is quite abstract. The reading of rhythm is, therefore, clearly the place to begin teaching the comprehension of printed music notation.

At this point, it is essential that teachers thoroughly understand four familiar terms used in discussing music and its movement— *beat, tempo, meter,* and *rhythm.* The beat is the underlying pulse which moves on evenly throughout the music; tempo refers to the rapidity with which the beat occurs; meter is the arrangement of the beats into groups of strong and weak pulsations; rhythm, in the strict sense, is the pattern of tones of varying duration which is superimposed over the basic underlying pulse or beat. True, these four terms are sometimes lumped together and referred to as the rhythm, but clarity demands they be separated.

During the music-reading readiness period, the children should have experienced a number of rhythmic activities which began to develop a strong feeling for the beat, for various tempos, and probably for a sense of meter. Until at least the feeling for a regular beat is established, it is folly to try to solve rhythm patterns. Probably the most common rhythmic deficiencies stem from a weak sense of beat. Children who can respond, speak, and play as outlined on page 14 are ready for the next step in music notation— presentation in a visual form of elements that are already familiar from the aural and kinesthetic standpoint.

Quarter notes and eighth notes should be presented simultaneously in the following manner: The teacher should place upon the blackboard a row of nine quarter notes with eighteen eighth notes beneath them.

The use of this number of notes is convenient because the pattern is long enough to emphasize the development of eye movement from left to right and is also adaptable to duple and triple meter.

The teacher should explain to the children that since they are proficient in playing and chanting walking and running notes, they should now *see* what these notes look like. The teacher should go through each line of notes at a moderate tempo, pointing to each note and chanting the appropriate word—*walk* or *run*. He should be careful to keep a strict two-to-one relationship between the eighth notes and the quarter notes. The children should be invited to join the teacher in chanting the lines of notes.

At this point, the children should be told the legitimate music names of the notes—quarter and eighth. Although the words *walk* and *run* will be used for some time to express movement of rhythmic patterns, the traditional music terms should be frequently used from the onset.

This first music-reading lesson should also include some of the following activities. The remaining should be taken up at the second or third lesson.

1. Various children in the class should come to the board and, as the teacher has already demonstrated, point along the rows of notes while the rest of the class chants "walk-walk" or "run-run."
2. The teacher may play on a drum one of the lines of notes and ask certain children to point to the line he is playing. The child should then follow along the line as the teacher plays.
3. The children should play on rhythm instruments portions of each line the teacher indicates. The pattern might be something as follows:

The purpose of this activity is to establish firmly the two-to-one relationship.

4. The children should open their music books and find examples of quarter and eighth notes.
5. There should be discussion of the various ways quarter and eighth notes are printed in books—

6. The class should be given instruction in how to draw quarter and eighth notes and should have opportunity to write some on paper and on the board.
7. The children should express, in physical motion, portions of each line of notes. That is, the teacher might write on the board ♩ ♩ ♩ ♩ ♩ and ask some child to move as the notes ask. The correct motion would be, of course, walk-walk-walk-walk-walk. The rest of the class might chant or play on instruments at the same time. In this activity, we are again emphasizing the expression rhythm through physical motion.

After two or three brief periods of these activities, stretched over a few days, the class should have a fairly clear understanding of the relationship between quarter and eighth notes from both the aural and visual standpoints. The next step is easily accomplished—chanting, playing, and stepping simple combinations of these notes.

Teachers may wish to use, for the first patterns to be solved, some of the following fragments:

The patterns should be short, easily grasped, and simple enough to be expressed easily in actual physical motion by walking and running. It is always astonishing how easily children can solve these simple rhythmic patterns if they have had a solid period of music-reading readiness. Within a very few music lessons after the introduction of visual notation, a second-grade class can read correctly the rhythmic notation of a short song which utilizes quarter and eighth notes.

As these first lessons in the reading of rhythmic notation are begun, another activity should be introduced. Music instruction at all levels of accomplishment involves training the ear, or improving the pupil's aural perception. Ear training has been an important part of the music-reading readiness work, and it should now be extended to an activity which is perhaps unique in elementary school music—taking rhythmic dictation.

Thomas Whitney Surette, one of the editors of the noted *Concord Series*, used to refer to this aspect of music education as the training of "the seeing ear and the hearing eye." That is, as one scans a printed page of music, he should be able to hear, to some extent, the sounds which are symbolized there. Conversely, as one hears music, he should be able to visualize its notation. Having now begun to teach him how to translate the printed page into sound, the teacher can improve the child's ability to do this by the reverse process—teaching him to write down the sounds he hears.

It has already been mentioned that children should learn to draw quarter and eighth notes during the first music-reading lesson. The teacher should give thoughtful attention to this activity, carefully showing how to draw and fill in the head, how to add the stem, and how to place the bar or flag to indicate eighth notes.

After the class can draw notes with some facility, it is an easy step to the first rhythmic dictation.

The dictation should be preceded by some explanation of what is being attempted—to see if the children can write down what the music says or does. A suitable pattern for the first dictation would be as follows: ♩ ♩ ♩ ♩. Here the child has but two problems—deciding whether the notes are walking or running (which should be at once apparent) and *remembering* how many "walks" were played. This development of tonal memory is an essential part of ear training, and the first few attempts at rhythmic dictation should concentrate on this simple, but important, problem.

As soon as the children have begun to read rhythmic patterns involving both quarter and eighth notes, they should attempt to take these in dictation. They might begin with ♩ ♩ ♫ ♩, ♩ ♫ ♩ ♩, or ♫ ♩ ♩ ♩. Patterns that start with quarter notes are easier because the beat note is clearly established at the beginning.

An important factor in the development of ear training is repetition. The children should have many opportunities to return to dictation patterns they have attempted before, easy ones as well as those which have been found to be difficult. There must be a high degree of success in this ear-training work; otherwise, discouragement and disinterest may dampen the morale of the class.

Again, it must be pointed out that the teacher will need to see clearly the role of these music-reading activities in the total elementary music program. As interesting as music reading may be to the teacher, it should not become the basis of the music class in elementary school. Teachers are often tempted to make it so.

These initial music-reading lessons, including the dictation, are likely to be quite successful. Teachers become overly enthusiastic and begin to push on too quickly to more complex reading and dictation. They envision their students as soon being able to master rather complex scores; they see themselves as the teachers of a host of young musical geniuses. In the face of this success in music theory, less and less time is given to the original premise—raising the child's level of musical accomplishment through active participation.

The regular reviewing of favorite songs, learning new songs, and creating songs should be continued by the class as before. There should be no abatement of rhythmic activities or music listening. To do so is to bring about the school program so often singled out as one in which there is no joyous experience in making music. Let us never sacrifice the love of music in order to teach children to read notes. Young teachers often ask how much time should be devoted to formal music reading. It is, of course, difficult to say, but probably not more than a quarter of the total amount of time allotted to music should be devoted to reading activities. Any extension of this percentage should be viewed with great caution.

Now that the first steps in the music-reading program have been taken, the teacher is faced with the problem of continuing the work steadily and methodically. Half notes may be introduced soon and chanted with the word *Slow-o*. Dotted eighth and sixteenth note combinations ♪.♪ have been familiar for some time from the aural and kinesthetic standpoints. As soon as it seems wise, they should be part of the reading material. The word for chanting ♪.♪ is *Skipty*. Teachers may also wish to include whole notes, dotted half notes, and the quarter rest. The following table of notes may be considered sufficient material for rhythm reading and dictation through the third grade and, in some situations, through the first half of the fourth grade:

♩	quarter note	chanted as	Walk
♫	eighth notes	chanted as	Run, run
♩	half note	chanted as	Slow-o
♪.♪	dotted eighth and sixteenth notes	chanted as	Skipty
♩.	dotted half note	chanted as	Hold-2-3
o	whole note	chanted as	Stop-2-3-4
‖	quarter rest	chanted as	Rest

Teachers should use this material in many ways by constructing patterns for reading, dictating simple combinations, and permitting children to move through space in expressing the notes and patterns derived. It is very worthwhile to do simple drills from the blackboard which involve patterns that will soon appear in the children's songbooks. It is absolutely essential that all of these notes be given the proper relationship in time value to a quarter note. To accomplish this learning, the metronome is most helpful; the following procedure may serve as an example.

A metronome of the traditional Seth-Thomas swinging-arm type should be brought to the class. It might be explained as a walking machine which will produce a steady stream of notes which are perfectly even. By moving the weight of the arm up and down, the children may be shown how the machine can walk slowly, moderately, rapidly, or even run. By setting a tempo ♩ = 100, an average walking pace for children can be established, and individuals and small groups may try walking about the room while others clap in time with the ticking.

Eventually, most of the class should be able to clap their hands or play on rhythm instruments a steady succession of quarter notes as marked out by the metronome. The tempo should be varied occasionally from ♩ = 60 to ♩ = 120. The next step should be to set the metronome ticking quarter notes at about ♩ = 72 and have the children clap, play, and chant *half* notes, performing on every other tick. A little work of this sort sharpens the children's rhythmic perception tremendously. The work should then move to performing in various order all the other notes given in the table above. The teacher may proceed along these lines—"Now, children, let us chant quarter notes,"

Walk   Walk   W   W

"half notes,"

Slow - o Slow - o S - o

"quarter notes," . . . . "eighth notes," . . . . "quarter notes," etc. In order to re-establish the relationship to the basic pulse, there should be a return to the chanting of quarter notes between each new series attempted.

By the beginning of the fourth grade, the children will have sufficient rhythmic reading vocabulary to enable them to work out many of the songs in the school's basic music series books. During the course of the year, the teacher may decide that the class is ready for dotted quarter and eighth notes. This rhythmic pattern is vastly more complex than anything attempted before; the problem arises from the fact that there is a lack of movement on the beat following that upon which the dotted quarter is sounded. In teaching the pattern, the teacher must be very sure that the children feel the beat which occurs at the time of the dot.

The pattern should be presented in the middle of a flow of quarter notes, which will establish the beat.

The dotted quarter note may be chanted as a *step* note, emphasizing the *ep*; the eighth note is already familiar as *run*. The pattern given above, therefore, would be chanted as

walk,   walk,   ste -*ep*,   run, walk,   walk,   walk.

The step note can be expressed by the usual walking motion with a little dip or bending of the knee at the time of the dot. In clapping the pattern, the hands may be struck together on the dotted quarter note, dropped downward in a quick motion on the following beat, and brought up again in time for a quick clap on the eighth note. The important thing to accomplish is the expression of physical motion on the beat where no new note is sounded. The pattern should at once be located in familiar songs; "America" and "America the Beautiful" are helpful.

It is not necessary, during the first four grades, to involve the children in a detailed explanation of meter, meter signature, measures, or the mathematical relationships of notes. The emphasis should be, rather, upon the development of a strict sense of beat, expressed in quarter notes. There should be a long period of aural experience in relating notes of different time values to the underlying quarter-note pulse, which, in turn, should be experienced at different tempos. The "tyranny of the bar line" has been long with us, and students will grow to have a better concept of musical phrase and line if their thinking is not too soon compressed into three- and four-beat units.

At some point, perhaps in the fourth grade, children may ask for some explanation of the bar line and the time signature. (The latter might better be termed the *measure* signature.) If it is necessary, a measure may be explained truthfully as a device which helps us find our place in a long line of music notes. The signature gives us a picture of each measure—2/4 means that each measure contains two quarter notes, or the equivalent. Children should, by this time, be thoroughly aware of the aural and visual equivalence of two *walking* notes—four *running* notes or one *slow-o* note.

The traditional definition of the measure signature as a sign which indicates that "there are so many beats in a measure and that such and such a note gets one beat" should be avoided. This explanation is almost meaningless in our presentation of music reading because we have not considered any but the quarter note as the note which functions as the beat note.

Sometime during the fourth grade, at about the same time that bar lines and meter signatures are discussed, the music teacher will find it valuable to teach the children something about the traditional time-beating patterns of the conductor. In these days of educational television, the orchestra conductor is a most familiar figure; school concerts by instrumental groups are far more common than they were even ten years ago; some prominent conductors today are as well-known to young people as national heroes in sports.

An understanding of the conducting patterns for music in 2/4, 3/4, and 4/4 will do much for the children's comprehension of measures and meters. As the class conducts familiar songs in these meters, the stress of the downbeat will be both *seen* and *felt*. By conducting recordings of orchestral music, the importance of accent on the first beat of the measure will become clear.

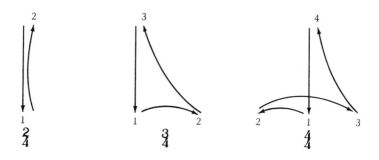

As music reading is continued in the fifth and sixth grades, teachers will find that conducting is a valuable device for creating additional interest in music study. Girls and boys in these grades should have many opportunities to conduct singing and instrumental music. As the studies in dynamics (Chapter 5) are taken up, the function of the left hand may be explained also.

Rhythm reading involving half, eighth, or dotted eighth notes as the beat note should not be attempted until the fifth or sixth grade, depending upon the overall musical development of the class. Compound rhythms are vastly more complex, and the music teacher should not attempt to teach them until a great deal of security in reading simple rhythms has been gained. The teaching of 6/8, 9/8, etc. will be discussed in Chapter 6.

Elementary school music programs which give some attention to teaching children to read music are usually taught by music teachers who have had vocal studies as the basis of their musical training. Although their singing lessons have probably been supplemented by keyboard instruction, they are not likely to be very familiar with other musical instruments. The use of simple classroom instruments is usually taken up in elementary music methods classes, but the idea of extensive instrumental exploration in the grades is usually relegated to a special instrumental instructor.

Here, possibly, lies one of the greatest weaknesses in our elementary school music program. Lacking knowledge of what the other is attempting, the vocal teacher and the instrumental teacher often go their own ways. The instrumentalist very often feels that the vocal classes are aimed largely at recreation and entertainment; the vocal teacher accuses the instrumental teacher of being interested only in a selected group of talented children.

One way that this disagreement can be overcome is by bringing more instrumental experiences into the general elementary music class. To do so improves both the vocal and the instrumental programs. The use of instruments is an excellent way to solidify the children's music-reading ability.

In our readiness program, we gave considerable attention to playing simple classroom instruments as accompaniment to songs. This work should be continued at least through the fourth grade; in addition, there should be emphasis on reading notation for rhythm instruments. We began playing our first visual pattern (p. 26) on instruments. If this study is regularly continued, it is but a short move to something like this:

Triangle, Sticks *etc.*

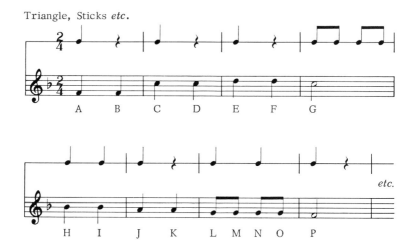

Large charts of this nature should be used with familiar songs and with very easy rhythmic accompaniments placed above the melody as illustrated. The class may sing the song, then practice the accompaniment. Combining the two activities really presents no great problem to the children.

After security has been gained through considerable experience with this activity, the song and the accompaniment should be separated into different cards and placed so both cannot be seen at the same time. Two groups may then perform—one singing and the other playing. Each must listen to the other and read his music at the same time. Eventually, two or three lines of rhythmic accompaniment to a song may be included. As was mentioned under the readiness program, the overall texture must not become too thick. In the case of "Twinkle Twinkle Little Star," the following complexity should probably be sufficient:

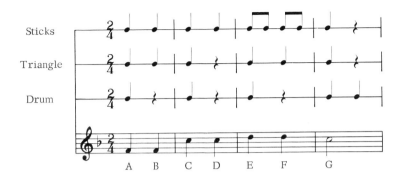

In a similar fashion, the teacher should construct simple rhythm accompaniments to short piano pieces and give the children opportunities to play on rhythm instruments while he plays the piano. Again, the music should not be too complex, and it certainly should be of the highest quality. Minuets of Bach, Haydn, and Mozart are excellent, as are the short piano pieces of Chopin, Schumann, and Schubert. Contemporary compositions should also be used. Rhythmic accompaniments to live performances at the piano are preferable to playing with recordings.

Some very worthwhile work may be done on rhythm instruments if the teacher can compose some short pieces for rhythm instruments alone. Only three or four varieties of sound should be attempted. With this number, a group of children can be arranged as a trio or quartet. Under these conditions, each child can hear the others well and still concentrate on his own part. These rhythmic compositions should be worked out by the teacher in score form first, then each part should be copied onto a large chart. If desired, or if it seems necessary, each part may be practiced separately by the whole class before the entire composition is attempted.

Only the teacher himself, who is constantly evaluating the music-reading growth of the class, can determine the proper complexity of these rhythmic compositions. For this reason, it is far better that the rhythmic compositions practiced by the class be composed especially for them. Progress in reading rhythmic notation depends to a very great extent on the ability of the teacher to discern the problems at hand and to produce studies which will remedy the situation.

Thus far, mention has been made only of the use of rhythm instruments. The following chapters will discuss the ways in which instruments of definite pitch may be employed in the music-reading program. Needless to say, playing a fixed pitch instrument is considerably more difficult than anything hitherto attempted.

For the sake of clarity, this chapter has been limited to a survey of rhythm-reading problems usually encountered in the second, third, and fourth grades. The reading of pitch, discussed in the next chapter, will also be started in the second grade. It is a far more difficult problem, however, and should not be attempted in depth until ample security in translating rhythmic notation has been established.

SUMMARY

Experiences which produce growth in rhythm reading:

1. Chanting lines of quarter and eighth notes from the blackboard with the words *walk* and *run*, respectively.
2. Learning the legitimate musical names of walking and running notes.
3. Playing lines of quarter and eighth notes from the blackboard on rhythm instruments.

4. Experiencing the rhythmic relationship of quarter and eighth notes.
5. Finding quarter and eighth notes in music books.
6. Drawing quarter and eighth notes.
7. Solving simple rhythmic patterns which contain both quarter and eighth notes.
8. Expressing simple rhythmic patterns in physical motion.
9. Learning to take simple rhythmic dictation.
10. Discovering half, dotted eighth and sixteenth, dotted half, and whole notes. Experiencing the quarter rest.
11. Learning rhythmic patterns in different tempos with the help of the metronome.
12. Reading the rhythm of complete songs from music books.
13. Becoming aware of measures and measure signatures.
14. Learning to conduct.
15. Reading rhythmic accompaniments to familiar songs.
16. Performing compositions for rhythm instruments alone.

SUGGESTIONS FOR FURTHER STUDY

ELLISON, Alfred. *Music with Children.* New York: McGraw-Hill, 1959. Pages 42–44.

GARRETSON, Robert L. *Music in Childhood Education.* New York: Appleton-Century-Crofts, 1966. Pages 56–57, Chapter 5.

RUNKLE, Aleta, and ERICKSEN, Mary LeBow. *Music for Today's Boys and Girls.* Boston: Allyn and Bacon, 1966. Pages 88–92, 126–137.

SWANSON, Bessie. *Music in the Education of Children,* 2nd ed. Belmont, Cal.: Wadsworth, 1964. Pages 87–98.

Chapter 4

Reading Pitch

WHEN CHILDREN are given regular, carefully directed experiences in reading rhythm, the teacher can expect a considerable amount of success. Rhythmic patterns can be clearly expressed in many ways—by chanting, clapping, or in actual bodily movement through space. Rhythm, therefore, can be expressed in a tangible form which can be visually demonstrated, explained, and discussed. Children who, at the outset, seem to have marked rhythmic deficiencies improve rapidly in their comprehension of rhythm reading.

On the other hand, pitch is quite intangible. Explanations of pitch are entirely dependent upon the ability of the ear to hear the pitch. It has been demonstrated many times that children and adults alike possess an inborn ability to distinguish between pitches and that this ability varies greatly from person to person. There are people who can sing any pitch named without reference to an instrument, and there are those who, indeed, cannot tell up from down.

Our very terminology regarding changes of pitch is possibly wrong, or at least confusing to children. When a tone changes from C to D, we may state that the pitch has gone up, yet nothing has actually moved in any direction except possibly certain parts of the instrument producing the tone. In the case of a bell lyre, the mallet has certainly gone up higher on the bars, but the hand moves *sideways* to the right on the piano, and *down* on the cello. The whole discussion can be an absolute mystery to children, especially when the demonstration is limited to tones demonstrated by the voice alone, which can produce an infinite number of pitches.

This is not to suggest that we abandon our current pitch terminology. After all, what would choral conductors do if they could not accuse their singers of being "flat"? There are, however, at least two important considerations for our program of teaching children. During the early stages of teaching pitch (1) any demonstration or discussion of pitch should be accompanied by a *visual* representation of the pitch change which is taking place, and (2) any reading of pitch notation should not be limited to reproduction by the voice alone, but should include experience on an instrument of fixed pitch, such as bells, the piano, or the organ.

Some visual representation of changes in pitch should be included in the first rote songs presented in the early grades. The simplest and possibly the most effective way is for the teacher to indicate the rise and fall of the melody with his hand. The lowest note of the song is indicated by a position of the hand at slightly above waist level; the highest tones, at eye level. With these simple motions, children are often assisted in learning tunes which, at first, seem elusive. The teacher may, at times, sing melodies and ask the children to indicate the direction of the tune as it moves from note to note. Children should also have opportunity to practice this exercise while the teacher plays melodies on the piano, bells, or other instruments.

In recent publications, a number of music educators have emphasized the use of hand signals to indicate the different steps of the scale. These hand signs have long been used by European music teachers and provide a way to indicate a specific pitch, once a home tone or key has been located. Hand signs are an important part of the Kodaly method and have been shown to be a valuable visual aid to pitch teaching. All music teachers should be familiar with them.

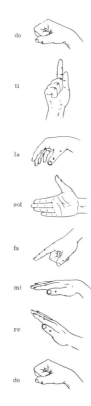

Until quite recently, the organ has not been used to any extent in school music classes. The parlor organ of the late nineteenth century has become a collector's item; pipe organs are, for the most part, inaccessible; and music teachers recoil in horror from the tones of the electronic organ.

Yet, the electronic organ offers many advantages over any other instrument which can be used in the elementary music class. It remains in tune, and small organs can be easily moved from room to room. A keyboard instrument is capable of playing either melodies or accompaniments, and a person may sing while playing. The keyboard clarifies such theoretical concepts as half steps, whole steps, tetrachords, and triads better than any other instrument. While, of course, the piano provides all of these advantages, the electric organ has a further asset—it produces sustained tones.

Sustained tones from wind instruments, strings, and voices account for a substantial part of our musical experiences. Sustained tones should form the foundation of the child's early musical experience, and the organ will provide this in the elementary classroom. Using a simple registration of flute and string tones, the teacher can play melodies with simple accompaniments which will greatly improve the singing of the class. *Legato style,* the basis of all beautiful singing, receives a tremendous impetus from a constant use of the organ. While the piano can indeed be a valuable instrument in elementary music activities, its percussive tone is not the best accompaniment for children who are learning to sing.

During the music-reading readiness period, the teacher should give close attention to the development of the children's singing voices. As the repertoire of the class grows, there should be a marked improvement in the quality and range of the young voices. Children who are insecure in pitch will probably improve considerably by themselves, but it may be necessary to give individual help in tone matching. At any rate, before the program in pitch reading is begun, most of the children in the class should be able to sing simple melodies within a range of five or six notes. Depending upon the maturity of the class, the amount of time devoted to musical activities in kindergarten and the first grade, and depending upon various other circumstances, mid to late second grade seems to be an appropriate time to begin the pitch-reading program. This work should not be started until after some security in rhythm reading has been gained.

The first step in pitch reading is to establish the concept of key and to feel the relationship of near-by tones to the *key tone,* or *tonic.* The customary systems of vocal music reading (use of syllables or numbers) work toward this objective. The student learns that a certain tone is *home,* or tonic; this tone is either called *do* or *one.* The remaining tones of the scale are given other names or numbers, and the student slowly learns the aural relationships. Whether to use numbers or syllables to teach this relationship is often a perplexing question for young teachers. Both will accomplish the desired end; both have advantages and disadvantages.

Numbers are at once meaningful to young children; interval study is clarified by the use of numbers. Syllables are not meaningful to children, but they encourage better singing sounds; when chromatic tones are introduced later, syllables can be easily altered to cover the situation. Which system to use must be the decision of each teacher. It is not wise to try to teach both systems; to do so is to waste time and to confuse the children. Numbers may have a slight advantage over syllables in that they are already well within the child's general experience. Chromatics can be handled in ways which eliminate such objectionable and awkward rhythmic distortions as attempting to sing "one, two, three, *four-sharp,* five." For this reason, numbers will be used in this book to teach pitch relationships. However, teachers who prefer to use syllables will find no difficulty in adapting each pitch study to their own teaching method.

With appropriate discussion and class participation, the teacher may begin the pitch-reading lessons by drawing on the board a five-rung ladder; the numbers *one* through *five,* or the syllables *do* through *sol,* should be placed as shown.

5		Sol
4		Fa
3	*or*	Mi
2		Re
1		Do

The teacher should demonstrate the sound of the ladder by

singing the numbers or syllables slowly and clearly, pointing to each number or syllable as he sings the first five tones of a major scale. It is not necessary to use any particular pitch for *one* or *do*, but the five tones should lie in a comfortable part of the child's voice. The children should join the teacher in singing up and down the ladder; the movement should be without skips. Little by little the teacher should cease singing and merely point to the notes as the class sings.

If the students seem to be doing well in singing from *one* up to *five* and back, the teacher may try holding one of the tones and then jumping back to *one*. If this is successful, the class may try leaping from *one* up to *five* and back to *one* or attempt to follow the teacher's hand as he pauses in the midst of the ladder, changes direction, and holds or repeats notes. The children will enjoy this game and, as the activity is reviewed during the course of several lessons, they should gain considerable familiarity with the first five tones of the major scale, identifying each tone with a number and visually relating the tones to the up and down motion of the hand.

The natural inclination of the teacher at this point is to add at once the remaining tones of the scale to complete the octave. To do so, however, is to present several much more difficult problems, most of which should probably wait for some months. The first five tones of the major scale are quite easy for children to remember, especially when the pitches are associated with numbers. The *one* and the *five* form a convenient boundary to the tonal area under exploration; the *three*, lying in the middle of this space, is a reliable guidepost to *two* and *four*. The tones lying above the dominant are not nearly so easy to hear. *Six* is strongly attracted to *five*, and *seven* wishes to rise to tonic, so the distance from *six* to *seven* seems greater than other whole steps in the scale. If children are required to sing melodies which leap from the lower part of the scale to *six* or *seven*, there is likely to be some confusion in a momentary loss of aural orientation to tonic and dominant. It is far better to leave the upper tetrachord of the scale until after the children have thoroughly mastered the lower five tones.

The tones *one* to *five* should be thoroughly drilled in as many ways as the teacher can construct. Some approaches which will interest the children are as follows:

1. Using the numbers on the ladder, the teacher points to a sequence of numbers which produces a familiar melody.

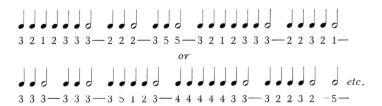

3 2 1 2 3 3 3—2 2 2—3 5 5—3 2 1 2 3 3 3—2 2 3 2 1—

or

3 3 3—3 3 3—3 5 1 2 3—4 4 4 4 3 3—3 2 2 3 2 —5—

2. The numbers may be written in a line moving from left to right in sequences which will produce easily sung melodies.

1	2	3	4	5	5	5__
5	4	3	2	1	1	1__
1	2	1	2	1	3	5__
5	4	3	2	1	1	1__

This rhythmic pattern may be used to construct a great number of simple, five-tone melodies. The children themselves should construct some tunes, different children adding lines of melody to a first line given by the teacher. Some children will show a remarkably creative ability at constructing entire songs of five tones within this simple rhythmic structure.

Very soon after the children have begun to sing with numbers, ear training with pitch dictation should be started. At first, the teacher may play simple two- and three-note patterns on the piano, asking the children to name the numbers that are played. The patterns should start with *one* so that the children may, in these early stages, relate to a sounded tonic. The following patterns may serve as an example for these first dictations:

Key of C   1 2 1 / 1 2 3 / 1 1 2 / 1 3 2

               1 3 5 / 1 5 3 / 1 5 4 / 1 5 2

The class as a whole may answer the teacher by singing back the numbers he has played. The teacher may, at times, call for a response from individuals. Although there is always the danger of pupils being embarrassed, girls and boys in the second and third grades usually enter into this dictation activity quite freely. The teacher certainly should ascertain, as soon as possible, which children are having difficulty. The early stages are best for remedying difficulties in comprehending pitch.

When the majority of the class can sing the correct numbers to short tonal patterns played by the teacher, the students should then attempt to *write* the numbers after the pattern has been played. After the children have gained facility in writing patterns or sequences of three or four notes, the length of the dictation should be slowly increased to perhaps seven or eight notes. Expanding the children's tonal memory is an important goal of this activity.

Additional interest in these ear-training activities may be developed by having the children take turns in giving the dictation. Those children showing special abilities may like to play or sing patterns for the rest of the class to write down or sing back. Often, the less secure child will profit greatly from an occasional opportunity to lead.

Soon it may be possible to add scale steps *six, seven,* and *eight.* This addition should be made gradually, with *six* being presented as closely related and attracted to *five* and with an attempt to feel the four tone pattern *five–six–seven–eight* as a whole idea. If the class grasps the idea of *eight* as a sound which is similar to *one,* it may be possible to add the three tones below the *one* to produce an extended ladder.

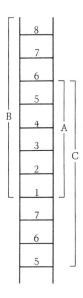

This extended series of tones will suffice for a long period of careful study and drill. The area encompassed by the bracket "A" is, of course, the easiest and most familiar; the "B" area should be worked upon with concentration on the upper tetrachord; the "C" area, being the most difficult, will need the most practice. As with all the other aspects of reading music, gaining a full comprehension of this scale ladder can only be accomplished by slow, steady progress. A most important factor is the constant return to the areas which are very secure (usually the "A" section); the class may then proceed to the new or less familiar areas. By the end of the fourth grade, a class which has had carefully organized instruction will be able to sing up and down this extended ladder as the teacher points to the numbers. Skips of up to a fifth should be possible. If there is a momentary loss of key orientation on scale steps *two, four, six,* and *seven,* the children should be able to locate the sound by reference to *one, three, five,* or *eight,* which must be very secure.

As the children gain more familiarity with the extended scale ladder and as they are able to sing number melodies of greater complexity, the teacher should plan to introduce the staff. This is a most important step and should be carefully thought through.

The basic problem lies in making clear to the children that tones are located on both the lines and the spaces. One way of presenting this information is as follows.

The teacher may prepare an illustration of a house with a sidewalk leading to it.

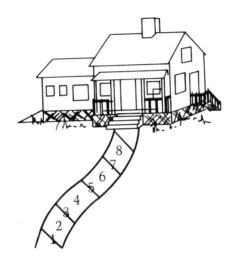

On the cracks and spaces of the sidewalk may be placed the eight tones of the scale, with *one* on the first crack. With a bit of explanation about playing "Step on the crack—break a monkey's back," the children will have little difficulty in understanding the concept of tones placed on lines and spaces. The cracks of the sidewalk may then be extended to form the five-line staff.

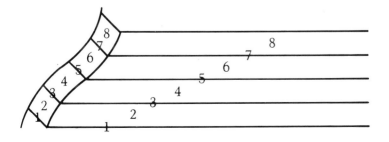

From this point, it is an easy step to singing number melodies directly from the staff.

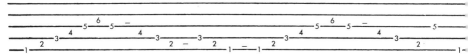

After facility is gained with this technique, the numbers may be enclosed by notes, then finally eliminated.

The teacher can create a useful device for drilling these initial stages of line and space reading by constructing from paper or cardboard a large note, with a cut-out space in the head.

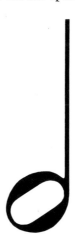

The teacher can use this cardboard note to improvise melodies merely by moving the note along some sort of permanent staff on the blackboard.

With this simple, time-saving device, regular practice of simple melodies and tonal patterns can be accomplished. The boys and girls themselves should have many opportunities to construct melodies with the cut-out note. In this way, the rather frequent problem of a student's inability to determine whether a note is on a line or on a space is usually completely solved.

By the time the children can read very simple melodies with the keynote located on the first line, it will be possible to combine some of the rhythm-reading work previously accomplished with the pitch reading. In so doing, we are presenting independent music reading for the first time. The initial work should be done first by reading very easy melodies in the key of E or E-flat major. It is better to use the blackboard for the music at this stage rather than individual books in the pupils' hands, for the teacher can more easily discern the ability of the individual students to grasp the instruction.

The teacher should attempt to find short, attractive songs for this first reading material. Books of folk songs will yield many lovely melodies with limited range and simple rhythmic patterns. The school's music series books may also offer good material for these first music-reading lessons. There is likely to be a scarcity of songs in the key of E flat or E, where the first independent reading takes place. Therefore, songs for these first reading lessons must often be transposed and notated on large sheets of illustration board which can be easily read by the entire class. Although a great deal of work is required in preparing these reading songs, they do become important elements of the music teacher's teaching equipment.

In presenting a new song for reading, the following outline of steps may be helpful:

Do You Hear

By permission of the Follett Publishing Company, from Book 2 of *Discovering Music Together* series.

1. The teacher should give appropriate introductory remarks which may motivate the class. Long, fanciful yarns, such as telling the class that he heard a bird sing this song on his window ledge that morning, are neither necessary nor valuable. There might be an explanation of the text which could be read to the children. *The teacher should not sing the song,* for children who have been learning the music activities described here are remarkably good at remembering the melody and might, therefore, never read the melody independently.

2. The teacher and pupils may look through the song to determine the kinds of notes to be found there, such as quarter notes or eighth notes. The class should then chant the rhythm of the entire song to the rhythmic words *walk, run,* etc. During this chant-

ing, it is wise for the teacher to conduct the traditional time-beating patterns given on page 34. After chanting the song with the rhythmic words, the teacher may have the class chant with a neutral syllable, such as *ta*, and/or read the words of the song in the rhythm which has been determined by the chanting.

3. Next, the song should be examined to determine the pitch numbers of the melody. The teacher may ask such pertinent questions of the class as "What is the number of the first note in the song?" "What is the number of the last note in the first line?" ". . . the third line?" Familiar tonal patterns may be pointed out, and any difficult skips should be mentioned.

4. The teacher should now orient the children to the key and practice passages that will help them when they actually begin to read the song. Attuning the class to the key may be accomplished by singing the keynote (E or E flat) and then requesting the class to sing passages such as 1-2-3-4-5 or 1-3-5-8. Some of the tonal patterns in the song may be reviewed at this drilling. This orientation to the key should be concluded by the singing of the keynote followed by the first note of the song. Proceed immediately to the next step.

5. While the teacher conducts, the class should sing the entire song with numbers in the correct rhythm. The teacher should not sing unless the reading threatens to break down, in which case he should come in to save the situation and then drop out when the reading goes better. A moderate tempo should be selected, and correct rhythm maintained. If there are several problems in the song, it is wise to sing the entire song again with numbers. If the reading has gone smoothly, the class should at once sing the melody with a neutral syllable such as *loo*. This done, they may proceed directly to singing the song with the text.

These five steps constitute an organized procedure which should be carefully followed while the children are in the early stages of independent reading. This procedure emphasizes the study of one thing at a time and the gradual acquisition of the skills of reading music. As more songs are studied and as the class improves its reading ability, the teacher may vary the procedure to some extent by omitting the chanting with rhythmic words, the rhythmic reading of the text, or the singing of the melody with a neutral syllable. The teacher must work diligently and thoughtfully to produce in the class a slow, steady growth in music-reading ability.

Very soon after the children begin to read simple songs in the keys of E or E-flat major, they should learn to play instruments. Playing instruments will stabilize the pitch and give them further experience with vocal and instrumental sounds together. Admittedly, playing in E or E flat is slightly more difficult than playing in C, but with the use of tone bars, the teacher can easily arrange the necessary notes for simple melodies in these keys. The most important thing to avoid at this time is a long, involved explanation of key signatures, sharps and flats, etc. This kind of material should be postponed to a much later time.

If a song in E flat is to be read, for example, the necessary tone bars may be arranged to form the scale:

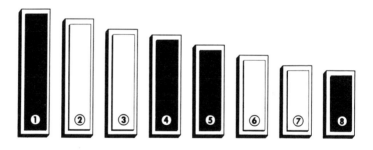

The children are, of course, playing only by numbers at this point; they have not yet learned the letter names of the staff. It is, therefore, necessary to affix numbers to the tone bars. Strong masking tape may be used for this purpose.

After using the tone bars in this manner, it is an easy step to a similar use of the organ or piano keyboard.

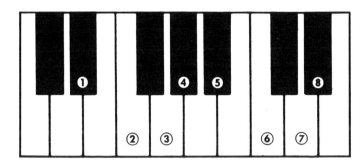

At first, the children may be able to play only certain sections of the song, such as reiterated tonal patterns, scale figures, or first and last notes. The eventual aim, however, is to play the entire song.

The initial music-reading lessons should concentrate on songs in the keys of E or E-flat major for a period of some weeks until the children have gained a fair degree of competence in those keys. It is not wise to attempt reading in other keys until an initial security has been gained. To remain too long, however, in keys whose *one* is on the first line will cause unnecessary problems, for the children often continue thinking in E or E flat after they have begun to study other keys. Something resembling elementary transposition sets in, and many difficulties arise. The plans for moving to new keys are discussed in Chapter 6.

In a school system with a well-directed plan for teaching music, the level of advancement and activities described in this chapter should be completed by the end of the third grade. Accomplishments will, of course, depend upon a number of factors familiar to all elementary teachers. The emotional, intellectual, and musical maturity of the students, the amount of time devoted to music in the classroom, and the teacher's interest in teaching music reading itself will all be contributing factors to the growth of the the children's comprehension. Yet, as in all the other aspects of music reading discussed, there is no more vital element in the reading program than the teacher's lucid analysis of the children's difficulties and his creative solutions for them. The continuum must be constantly surveyed, and the progress of the class thoughtfully evaluated.

SUMMARY

Experiences which produce growth in the reading of pitch:

1. Correlating rise and fall in pitch with visual representations of up and down.
2. Using the hand signs.
3. Singing melodies while instruments are played.
4. Singing the scale ladder with numbers or syllables.
5. Using numbers or syllables to sing familiar songs.
6. Singing and creating new melodies with numbers.
7. Taking melodic dictation.
8. Learning to sing number melodies from the staff.
9. Singing familiar and new melodies from the staff.
10. Learning a vocabulary of tonal patterns.
11. Recognizing tonal patterns in new songs.
12. Playing tonal patterns and very simple melodics on tone bars.
13. Reading very simple new melodies in E or E-flat major from the blackboard or from music books.

SUGGESTIONS FOR FURTHER STUDY

GARRETSON, Robert L. *Music in Childhood Education.* New York: Appleton-Century-Crofts, 1966. Pages 171–178.

NYE, Robert E., and NYE, Vernice T. *Music in the Elementary School,* 2nd ed. Englewood Cliffs, N. J.: Prentice-Hall, 1964. Pages 134–136, 303–316.

RUNKLE, Aleta, and ERIKSEN, Mary LeBow. *Music for Today's Boys and Girls.* Boston: Allyn and Bacon, 1966. Pages 79–88, 118–126.

Chapter 5
Reading Dynamic Indications

EXPRESSIVE, sensitive, musical performance is invariably characterized by careful attention to dynamic contrast. Except for *rubato,* dynamics provide the only significant means for a *musical* rendition of patterns of pitches and rhythms. Dynamic contrast is noticably absent in music performed by students, and even experienced musicians are likely to feel that one need give attention to *fortes, pianos, crescendos, forte-pianos,* and other expression marks only after the notes of a composition are well learned.

This tendency to "sprinkle on" the dynamic contrasts and other elements of expression during the last stages of musical study is most regrettable. It undoubtedly accounts for the vast numbers of student musicians who never reach the expressive stages and who always play or sing with a bland, *mezzo-forte* sound. True, a choral *fortissimo* or a real *pianissimo* by a wind ensemble is most difficult to achieve, but with only a small amount of instruction, elementary school children can gain a good understanding of the dynamic levels between *piano* and *forte*. This knowledge, together with some experiences in producing *crescendos* and *diminuendos*, will do much to eliminate the dull, unmusical renditions so common in elementary school music classes.

As with all aspects of teaching music, the example set by the teacher is of greatest importance. All children are sensitive to beauty until their ears and eyes are dulled by grossness. The teacher who always sings with the same blatant sound or who always pounds the piano to accompany the children's singing is doing much harm to their musical development. That teacher should not complain in later years if few of his students continue their musical activities.

Sensitivity to dynamics and general musical expressiveness should be stressed in the very first music classes. As was mentioned on page 12, a variety of tempos and moods should be expressed in the rote songs selected by the music teacher. The children will enjoy discussing why a lullaby, a march, or a song about snowflakes should sound a certain way. Songs with echo passages will provide early experiences with loud and soft renditions of the same melody. *Crescendo* and *diminuendo* can be demonstrated to children in songs about parades, trains, and other moving objects which come near and then move away.

Of even greater importance than these specific expression variants is the exposure of the children to sensitive and subtle changes in dynamic level. For example, while it is by no means an invariable rule of music performance that a *crescendo* always accompanies a rising melody, the concept is important enough to be sure that children understand it. Similarly, passages of exact repetition of notes should usually be performed at different levels of intensity; children can easily experience this technique.

In guiding the musical growth of young people, it is the duty of every vigorous, progressive music teacher to declare war on the insensitive, unmusical experiences foisted upon children in elementary school. The first musical activities in the lower grades should be marked by lovingly prepared renditions of beautiful songs for children. Such exemplary material will become the children's own, first by emulation and then by understanding. These early examples of musical expressiveness will become the foundation for a later development of aesthetic sensitivity. Coarse tone quality in singing, indifferent banging on pianos and other instruments, and scratched, worn-out records played on inferior reproducing equipment (to name but three common sins) can not but contribute mightily to the early breakdown of a young child's sensitivity to beauty.

The child's first experiences, therefore, in understanding dynamic contrasts, come simultaneously with his learning of beautiful and expressive rote songs in the kindergarten and first grade. Upon hearing his teacher sing various songs at different dynamic levels, he at first imitates the example given and then, hopefully, comprehends the need for general loud or soft rendition. Children should have an opportunity to discuss the mood of a song and to give suggestions for ways of singing it expressively. In the use of simple classroom instruments, children can gain further appreciation of loud and soft if they have a choice of various instruments, if they create appropriate rhythmic patterns of accompaniment, and if they play the instruments in a manner which enhances and complements the song.

During the music-reading readiness period, further experiences with dynamic contrasts can be undertaken as the children study rhythmic movement. Creative dramatizations, such as those mentioned on page 14, invariably call for the children to demonstrate several different ways of walking, running, and skipping. In dramatizing "Jack and the Beanstalk," for example, the walking sound of the Giant will differ markedly from that made by Jack. In supplying appropriate drum sounds for these two characters, the children will invariably choose a correct dynamic level.

It is hardly necessary to give further examples of ways in which children can be introduced to dynamic contrasts. The experiences of the class will be in direct proportion to the teacher's creative ability and interest in the activity. The point to be remembered is that before children can attach any real importance to a symbol such as *f*, *pp*, or ⎯⎯◁, there must be a wealth of experience with the actual result of such an indication.

The children's first observation of a printed symbol for a certain dynamic level of performance may come during his first experiences with the printed page of music. As tone-calls, phrases of the children's creation, and short songs are placed on the blackboard or on poster boards about the music room, the appropriate sign for loud or soft may also be given. If the children ask the meaning of the symbol, they should be told, for example, that *f* stands for *forte*, an Italian word meaning *loud*. The children should learn both the correct Italian pronunciation and the English meaning. The same procedure should be followed for *p—piano—*meaning *soft*.

During the music-reading readiness stage, attention to these two common dynamic indications will probably be sufficient. It will be especially effective if both marks can be encountered in the same song so the children will be able to practice changing the dynamic level. If the teacher has indicated a certain level of intensity for an appropriate rendition of a song, he should be sure that the children actually do perform the music in the prescribed manner. Musicians are, on the whole, terribly lax on this point.

As soon as the children begin to read rhythmic notation, as presented in Chapter 3, more dynamic and expression marks may be presented and utilized in different ways. As soon as the children begin to chant and play the rhythmic patterns given on page 28, they may have experience rendering the patterns softly or loudly. It is always interesting to have the children play the same rhythmic pattern at different dynamic levels while attempting to maintain the same tempo. Usually, the children will play more slowly while playing softly, and the teacher should guard against this error.

Some attention to dynamics should also be included in the earliest ear-training exercises. For example, when the rhythmic dictation exercises are begun, variety and interest may be obtained by creating some very easy dictations which include notating the dynamic level. The following may serve as examples for such studies:

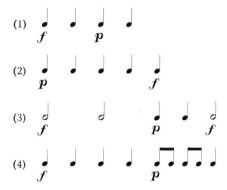

Once the *forte* (*f*) and *piano* (*p*) signs appear to be well understood by the children, the teacher may introduce the accent mark ＞ , the *crescendo* mark ⟨, and *diminuendo* ⟩. These five indications of expression, with the possible addition of *mezzo-piano* (*mp*) and *mezzo-forte* (*mf*), if conscientiously observed and utilized in the children's singing, rhythmic exercises, dictations, and instrumental study, will promote more musicality in the elementary music class than is usually found.

If the elementary vocal teacher carries out the work with rhythm instruments as described, beginning on page 36, many opportunities will arise for solidifying these studies in dynamic contrasts. The rhythm accompaniments to familiar songs and the additional parts for rhythm instruments to be used with piano pieces should be well marked with dynamics. The teacher should be careful that the children actually try to observe and carry out these dynamics as soon as they begin to study the pieces, rather than add them at a later time. If compositions for rhythm instruments alone are studied, correct execution of the dynamic indications will, of course, be essential to the musical performance of the pieces.

SUMMARY

Singing and playing in elementary school music classes are likely to be lacking in musical expressiveness. One way in which this deficiency can be overcome is to give careful attention to dynamic indications in the first songs which the children sing. As soon as the pupils begin to be familiar with printed music notation, the scores should contain some of the more familiar expression marks. Diligent and creative use of these symbols by the elementary music teacher can make them highly meaningful to his pupils. Through such work, some of the potential monotony of elementary school music classes may be avoided.

SUGGESTIONS FOR FURTHER STUDY

GARRETSON, Robert L. *Music in Childhood Education.* New York: Appleton-Century-Crofts, 1966. Pages 77–78.

RUNKLE, Aleta, and ERICKSEN, Mary LeBow. *Music for Today's Boys and Girls.* Boston: Allyn and Bacon, 1966. Pages 17–18, 220–222.

SWANSON, Bessie. *Music in the Education of Children,* 2nd ed. Belmont, Cal.: Wadsworth, 1964. Pages 191–192.

Chapter 6   Independent
Music Reading

IT IS NOT UNCOMMON to find elementary school music classes, particularly at the fourth and fifth grade level, which have achieved the minimal accomplishments in music reading. With the help of the music teacher, the class, *working as a whole,* can give a fairly accurate reading of a song comprised of simple rhythmic patterns and melodic intervals. Teachers of classes who have reached this level of ability are likely to feel that they have at least done something to combat the musical illiteracy of the elementary school. But too often, teachers do not go on beyond this point; the simple reading accomplishments of the primary grades are soon forgotten, and the few children who advance in understanding music notation are those who enter the instrumental program or some form of private instruction in music.

The purpose of this chapter, therefore, is to discuss some of the ways in which the music teacher can advance his classes from the basic reading accomplishments to a level where a high percentage of the children could be truly called independent music readers. Teachers are often wrong in their estimation of the reading ability of the class, because leaders soon begin to develop and the other students lean on the strong ones. Thus, the need to evaluate each child's music-reading ability becomes more and more important as the child enters the intermediate grades.

The level of accomplishment in music reading described in the preceding chapters can usually be attained by the time the children have reached the end of the third grade. The degree of security achieved will, of course, depend upon familiar factors involved in any learning situation—maturity of the students, general preschool background, the teacher's interest in the subject, and the regularity, thoroughness, and continuity of instruction. In accomplishing growth in music reading, probably no factor is more important to success than gentle persistence. If the music-reading program is progressing adequately, a child at the end of the third grade should, with but a little assistance from the teacher, be able to sing short melodies of roughly the following complexity:

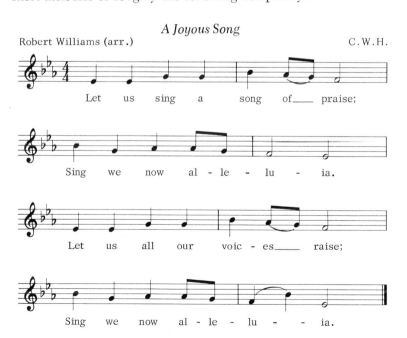

A Joyous Song

Robert Williams (arr.)   C.W.H.

With the help of numbers affixed to the instruments, he should be able to play isolated notes, fragments, or even the entire tune on bells or on a keyboard. The reading ability of the class *singing together* will probably be considerably in advance of this example. Appendix B, page   , will guide the teacher in evaluating the music-reading accomplishments of the average third-grade child.

The fourth grade is the ideal time to solidify the music-reading concepts begun in the primary grades. Music classes in the fourth grade should include much sight-reading of new songs, melodic and rhythmic dictation, and rereading of familiar songs. Not that reading music should become the main purpose of music in the fourth grade; far from it! But a focus on the study of music notation will bring a stronger sense of direction to the general plan of the music curriculum at this grade level. An emphasis on reading music will do much to unify the work being done in singing, rhythmic activities, listening to music, and creative music, as well as improve the relationship between the vocal and instrumental music programs.

Two important items in the music-reading continuum must be thoroughly mastered during the fourth grade. These items are (1) understanding the location of the keynote on any line or space of the staff, and (2) learning the letter names of the lines and spaces, including sharps and flats, with the resulting ability to locate on an instrument of fixed pitch any note which may appear in a song.

Learning to locate the keynote in any song. Many programs of music reading undoubtedly fail because of the large number of keys in which reading is attempted almost as soon as the children begin to translate music notation into sound. It is not uncommon to find songs in G, C, D, and F presented in rapid succession. Therefore, before the child has any facility in associating a particular syllable or number with a certain line or space, his orientation is changed. It is the same as a teacher of instrumental music presenting the problems of four or five different clefs within the first few months of instruction. Such teaching would be almost certain to fail, but vocal-music teachers are doing this when they regularly change the location of the keynote when the children are first learning to read.

The program of music reading advocated in this book calls for the first reading to be done with the keynotes, or *one*, being located on the bottom line of the staff; the first songs will then be in the key of E or E-flat major. Some teachers prefer to use only one of these keys. At any rate, the students should read in one or both of these keys until they have a reasonable grasp of the problems of music reading. They should develop a vocabulary of basic tonal patterns which they can quickly recognize and sing and play with assurance.

The point at which a new key should be introduced is sometimes difficult to ascertain. The move should not be made until the reading is secure in E or E flat. To remain too long in those keys, however, sometimes causes difficulty in moving to a new key.

It is recommended that the key of F major be studied next. The teacher should point out to the class that *one* may be placed on any line or space and that all the other numbers move along with it when *one* is moved. The teacher can easily illustrate this point by constructing a set of paper or cardboard notes as follows:

By moving the set of five notes (or a full octave of notes, if desired) the constant relationship of the notes can be clearly demonstrated. Once the point has been made, however, the class should concentrate for a time on the new key of F, with regular review of E or E flat.

The first reading in F should consist of very simple tonal patterns and phrases from the board, rather than a complete song from a book. The phrases should be constructed predominantly from small melodic intervals with considerable stepwise motion. As the children achieve success with this simple material, they may then attempt to read complete songs in F from their books. They should also become very fluent in reading the tonal patterns previously learned in E flat, but now transposed to F.

As the children grow in their ability to read in F and E flat, additional keys may be introduced as rapidly as the teacher desires. Once the concept of the relocated keynote has become familiar to the children, few difficulties will be encountered in presenting new keys. Once the key of F is well learned, the class may move quite soon to G, D, and C major. Mastery of these four keys, together with E or E-flat major, constitutes a goal to be reached by the end of the fourth grade.

Each new key should be studied from the instrumental standpoint as well as vocally, the procedure being essentially the same as that outlined on pages 54 and 55. For example, for playing in F major, the tone bars may be arranged as follows:

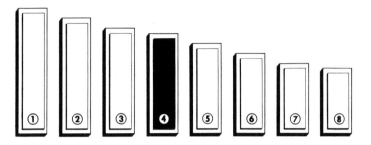

Or, a section of the keyboard could be set up with numbers attached to the keys.

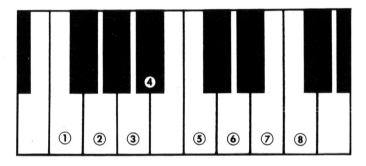

As the new keys are introduced, the children will undoubtedly ask how they can tell where to find *one*. In preparation for this question, the teacher should construct some rather large charts that show the correct key signature, the full octave of numbered notes, and the location of each note on the piano or organ keyboard. On the opposite page is a chart in the key of D major.

With these charts, the teacher will find that most children, merely by remembering the number of sharps and flats (terms which they should now learn) at the beginning of the staff, will be able to recall the position of the keynote. If it seems advisable, the following rules for locating the tonic note may be learned and practiced: To find *one* in the sharp keys, call the last sharp to the right in the key signature *seven;* having found the right place on the staff for *seven,* count down the lines and spaces to find *one* (Page 72).

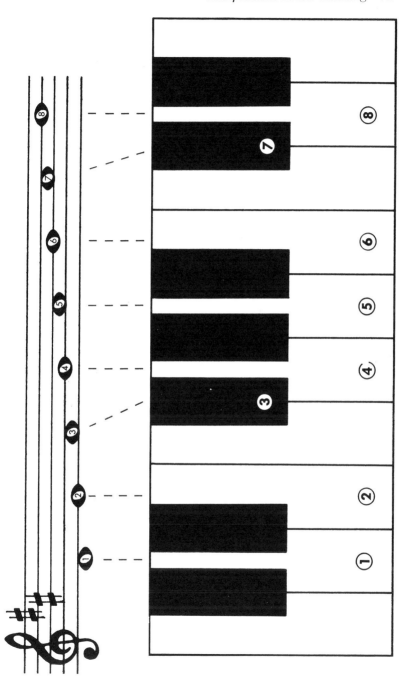

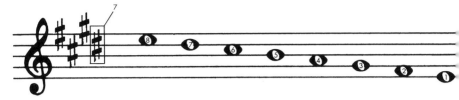

To find *one* in the flat keys, call the last flat to the right *four;* having found *four,* count down to find *one.*

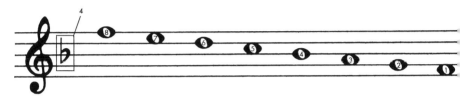

If there are no sharps or flats at the beginning of the song, *eight* is located on the third space; find *eight* and count down to *one,* which will be located on the first short line drawn beneath the staff.

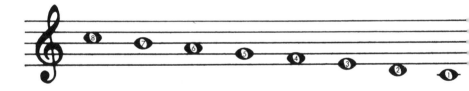

Learning the names of the lines and spaces of the staff. By the time students are able to read in two or three keys, they should learn the letter names of the lines and spaces of the treble staff. They should be able to locate on a keyboard any note (sharp or flat) which might appear in a song.

The names of the lines and spaces are most easily taken up in the fourth-grade music classes as the students begin reading in the key of C. The absence of sharps and flats will permit the teacher to explain the relationship of each line and space to the correct white key on the piano or organ. A large keyboard and staff placed on a chart will help the class learn the names of the keys.

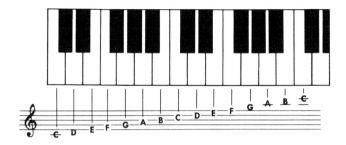

The members of the class should have many opportunities to play and sing isolated notes and short phrases from the songs that are being sung. After C major is well in hand, there may be a review of the keys containing two or three sharps or flats. In this way, the use of the black keys, already familiar through experience with number reading, may be reintroduced.

This use of the keyboard is one of the most important steps in the development of music-reading ability. Throughout the intermediate grades, music classes should constantly refer to the keyboard; its use can scarcely be over-emphasized. All the students should have their own printed cardboard keyboards, and the teacher must be sure that everyone in the class gets many opportunities to play the piano or organ.

The instrument, of course, *must* be in tune. The wide-spread insensitivity to pitch expressed by singers and instrumentalists in our schools probably has its beginnings in the elementary grades. Especially harmful to the development of reading ability is the piano which is tuned well within itself, but is *low in pitch throughout*. The A on a classroom piano must be tuned to within a few cycles of 440 vibrations per second. If the children have constant exposure to established pitch, many of them will be able to remember and sing the pitch associated with a particular letter. While cultivation of perfect pitch is not in any way the goal of our music-reading program, the use of numbers or syllables is to be gradually eliminated. If the students can begin to associate a certain pitch with a note on a specific line or space, their reading ability will progress all the faster.

During the fifth grade, three specific music-reading problems should be taken up and mastered: (1) singing accidentals, (2) reading by observation without the assistance of syllables or numbers, and (3) reading in two or more parts. If the reading lessons through the fourth grade have been thoroughly studied and learned, these three new reading problems will present no great difficulties.

Singing accidentals. The most common accidental in vocal music is the raised fourth scale step, as F sharp in the key of C major. The singing of accidentals may very well begin there. Before the class attempts to sing songs involving accidentals, the problem should be taken up in simple exercises with visual aids. Charts such as the following should be prepared:

Each of these examples should be sung slowly and clearly by the teacher, using the numbers *one* through *five*. In the second example, the *four* will be sung a half step higher. If pitches are being taught by syllables, *fi* should be substituted for *fa*. The class should then sing each example with the teacher as he points to each note. As the children are familiar with the names of the lines and spaces, sharps and flats, and their location on the keyboard, there will be little difficulty at this point in explaining and demonstrating these chromatically altered tones. It is extremely difficult for children to learn accidentals without knowing line and space terminology and without reference to an instrument of fixed pitch.

After the class has mastered the chromatic tones presented in the examples given above, or in other exercises devised by the teacher, a complete song utilizing the accidental may be studied. It is then a good plan to study songs in other keys that use the same altered step of the scale. For example, if the first accidental to be studied was the raised fourth degree of the scale, a song with F sharp in the key of C would be appropriate. After this chromatic has been successfully learned, the class might next read a song in F with a B natural, a song in G with a C sharp, or a song in E flat with an A natural. Through this procedure, the class will gain complete security with each chromatic tone as it is introduced.

Reading by observation. In Chapter 2, pages 20 to 22, the importance of reading by *observation* was discussed. As the children in the fifth grade increase their understanding of music notation, more and more attention should be given to this important aspect of reading vocal music. The class should, therefore, regularly attempt to sight-sing with a neutral syllable songs which are not too difficult, but which contain some of the rhythmic and melodic reading problems previously studied in detail.

Several factors should be carefully considered in preparing a lesson in observation reading:

1. The melodies should not be too difficult. It is far more beneficial for the students to read many melodies with a high degree of success than to struggle vainly with a few difficult problems.

2. After selecting a melody for observation, the teacher and the students should look through the song for possible problem spots, which should be discussed and solved. It is often beneficial to ask the class to sing isolated notes from the melody.

3. Before the students begin to read, the teacher must be sure to indicate the pitch of the first note and the tempo of the beat. The tempo and the pitch may be given simultaneously by intoning some preparatory directions on the pitch of the

first note. If the song begins with G on the first beat of a measure in 4/4 time, the teacher might sing:

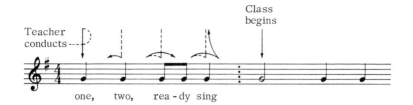

This pattern will need to be adjusted according to where the opening note of the song falls in the measure. If the first note is on the third beat of a 3/4 measure, for example, the preparation might be:

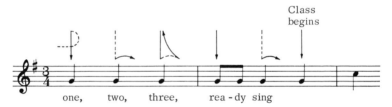

Almost any combination of numbers and prompting words may be employed in this preparation pattern so long as the meter and the tempo are clearly established on the correct pitch. The words "ready, sing" are useful because they establish the tempo of eighth notes.

Once the song has been started, the teacher should continue to conduct with a small, precise pattern. Even if some pitches are wrong, the rhythm must not falter. Every effort must be made to sing expressively and musically.

The growth of the class in its ability to read by observation should be the aim of the entire program of music-reading studies. The use of numbers to indicate pitches, rhythmic words to convey patterns of motion, and the many visual aids that have been mentioned are but so many means to a desired end. Regular, carefully prepared lessons in reading exercises and songs by observation should be an important part of the music-reading program from its very beginning.

Reading music in two or more parts.   Part singing is a logical outcome of growth in musical accomplishment. If the students are developing their skill in music reading and have a firm basis in musical experience, reading in parts will present no insurmountable problems.

Almost from the very beginning of their music-reading studies, the children should have been exposed to a variety of activities which convey the idea of several musical lines moving together in a complimentary manner. From early in the third grade, the music classes will have included songs with descants and *ostinati* as well as rounds and canons. Partner songs, which may be easily learned in the fourth grade, are most effective for presenting the concept of two independent vocal lines sung simultaneously. Playing instruments to accompany singing further develops the concept of musical texture.

Part singing, therefore, will be well within the children's experience before they start reading in parts. In preparing for the first lessons in two-part reading, several important factors concerning the musical development of the class should be considered:

1. Part reading should not be attempted until the class is quite proficient in unison reading. Part singing should not be the result of intensive drill of individual lines which, after being learned separately, are put together. For the most part, the class, divided into two groups, should be able to read the two parts simultaneously. Drill on troublesome intervals or rhythms may occasionally be necessary, but if the reading constantly bogs down or if the teacher is needed on one part or another to keep the song going, part reading should probably be postponed until the unison reading is more secure.

2. It is well to avoid the terms *soprano* and *alto* in discussing the two parts; children in the fifth grade should not be so labeled. The teacher may refer to the *first* and *second* parts or to the *higher* and *lower* parts. Under no circumstances should the same children

in the class always sing the higher or lower part. The temptation to put the best readers on the lower part is great. Many people have been incorrectly classified for life because of their childhood ability to sing a harmonic part. Ideally, all the children should have an opportunity to sing both parts in every part-singing lesson. In fact, if the members of the class can easily exchange parts, the teacher can be quite sure that good progress in reading is taking place and that the children are not merely learning the parts by rote.

3. A large portion of the part-reading work should be devoted to music of a contrapuntal, rather than harmonic, nature. Reading contrapuntal music develops independence much more rapidly and is actually easier, providing that rhythmic reading has been well taught.

4. Part reading should be begun with each part using numbers or syllables to determine the pitches; the correct pitch can thus be more easily ascertained. However, reading the parts by observation will do much for the children's reading development, interest in part singing, and sensitivity to pitch.

5. In so far as possible, the piano should be excluded from the part-reading work; emphasis should be placed upon careful listening to the *other part*. In *Let Us Sing Correctly*, Kodaly points out the necessity for singers to tune to other singers, rather than to the keyboard. His point is well made, and teachers would do well to examine his publication. Many of the exercises can be adapted for beginning part-reading classes.

6. As with most of the other aspects of music reading, the concept of two-part reading should be introduced through simple exercises from the board, rather than from the students' books. When reading from books, children are often helped by beginning with songs which have only a portion in parts and the remainder in unison. The part work may be found only in the chorus, at the final cadence, or in certain other places for special effect.

7. Once part singing has been introduced, many teachers are tempted to do no more reading in unison. This is probably a mistake, as there are always those children who are less proficient in reading and need the review of less complicated material. Rereading

familiar songs should continue to be an integral part of reading music.

Teachers must draw upon their creative abilities in devising interesting exercises for introducing two-part reading. The following may serve as an example:

Most of the current publications on music in the elementary school include helpful suggestions for introducing part singing—harmonizing by ear or singing chord patterns. The resourceful teacher will study these writings and incorporate their suggestions into his lessons. Part singing through a firm grasp of music notation is a significant accomplishment for girls and boys in elementary schools; every effort should be exerted to make this activity as exciting and rewarding as possible.

Near the end of the fifth grade or sometime near the beginning of the sixth, the music teacher may wish to introduce two or three final problems in music reading—reading compound rhythms, or rhythms that employ some note other than the quarter note as the beat note; reading in minor keys; and reading in three parts, with a special part for the boys whose voices are beginning to change. The first two problems cannot be really understood by children without a fair amount of musical sophistication; sixth grade classes do not often contain many boys whose voices are changing, but the problem merits attention because of its importance to vocal music in the junior high school.

Reading compound rhythms. The major problem in teaching

such rhythms as 6/8, 9/8, and 12/8, lies in the fact that the tempo of the composition has considerable bearing on the selection of the beat note. For example, "Drink to Me Only With Thine Eyes" is customarily notated in 6/8 rhythm. Each eighth note receives one beat. The song is conducted with this traditional pattern:

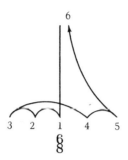

To read this rhythm, the students will need to adjust their thinking to a table of note values as follows:

$$\eighth = 1 \text{ beat}$$

$$\quarter = 2 \text{ beats}$$

$$\dottedquarter = 3 \text{ beats}$$

$$\dottedhalf = 6 \text{ beats}$$

$$\sixteenth = \tfrac{1}{2} \text{ beat}$$

With this table before the children, the teacher can prepare simple rhythmic exercises in 6/8 meter.

As with the rhythm reading in Chapter 3, the class should chant the patterns with *ta*, conduct the traditional pattern given above, and take dictation in this rhythm. A class with broad musical experience and ability in reading simple meters will quite easily learn this aspect of 6/8 time.

However, very little vocal music in 6/8 has six beats in a measure; it is much more common to feel *two* beats per measure with the dotted quarter note receiving the beat. The class then will need to understand that the beat note may be divided in different ways. For example:

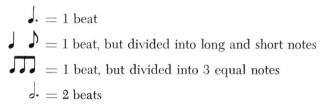

Rhythmic exercises of the following nature may then be constructed:

In order to understand clearly the solving of rhythmic problems in 6/8, the students must know how to attack the rhythmic patterns from both approaches—six beats to the measure and two beats to the measure. The following order of complexity in rhythmic reading is recommended as a procedure which will help children to gain a secure understanding of compound rhythms:

1. Reading songs in 3/8 at a slow tempo to establish the use of the eighth note as the beat note.
2. Reading songs in 3/8 at a more rapid tempo to accustom the children to dotted quarter notes as beat notes.
3. Reading songs in slow 6/8 rhythm; eighth notes receive the beat.
4. Reading songs in fast 6/8 rhythm; dotted quarter notes receive the beat.

5. Reading songs in moderate 9/8 and 12/8 rhythm; dotted quarter notes receive the beat.

Compositions in 6/8 rhythm are especially interesting to children because of the strong forward motion that the rhythm possesses. The ability to read and understand this rhythm is highly important to the child's musical development, and teachers must strive to present as lucid an explanation as possible.

Reading in minor keys. By the time children are in the fifth and sixth grades, they should be thoroughly acquainted with the sound of the minor mode. They will have sung songs in minor tonalities since the first or second grades, and they should have had some experiences in playing simple accompaniments in minor keys at about the fourth-grade level.

Indeed, some reading of melodies in the minor mode is possible in the late fourth or early fifth grades if the students are following the schedule of activities presented in this book. Students should find little difficulty in reading minor melodies of limited range, provided they encounter no accidentals. This limits the material to those minor songs whose range does not extend below the tonic or above the dominant in that particular key—from E to B in E minor.

However, most minor melodies include several chromatically altered tones, especially scale steps *six* and *seven*. It is very difficult to teach children how to read these melodies until the class knows the names of the lines and spaces, understands accidentals, can locate isolated tones on the keyboard, and is able to read by observation with some facility. Until these four skills have been gained, attempts at reading extended melodies will not be very successful.

Reading in minor keys is most easily mastered by children if the *relative minor scale* is studied in conjunction with the major key bearing the same signature. Having learned to read with numbers in major modes, the child can apply the same rules for finding *one*. Half steps will continue to fall between *three* and *four* and between *seven* and *eight*. The only new thing to be learned is the sensation of *six* as the tonic.

In preparation for teaching the first reading in minor, it is a good plan to teach a simple song in the relative major key first. E minor is a good key for the first minor reading, so the reading lesson may well begin with a simple song in G major. After this reading has been satisfactorily completed, the class should turn to a song in E minor. The following is excellent for beginners in reading minor melodies.

Good Night

Translated by Rev. Vincent Pisek   Czech Folk Song

From the collection *Twenty-Two Bohemian Folk Songs* by the Reverend Dr. Vincent Pisek. Reprinted by permission of the Jan Hus Church, 351 East 74th St., New York, N.Y. 10021.

With the key signature of one sharp, the class can locate *one* on the second line, as in the G-major song just completed. The first note is identified as *three;* the final note, as *six.* The class will easily read the song, needing only a bit of help from the teacher during the third line, where the tonality shifts momentarily from E minor to G major.

There will be some puzzled expressions as the song concludes on *six.* The teacher may then explain that songs ending on *six* are usually in minor keys, in contrast to major key songs, which usually end on *one* and sometimes end on *three* or *five.* The class should then look through an assortment of new songs to discover which are in major and which are in minor. Some time should be spent in reading simple songs, as the one printed above, before more advanced minor melodies with chromatically altered tones are attempted.

The most common accidental in minor mode is the raised seventh scale step—F sharp in G minor, for example. Before the class attempts to read complete songs containing this accidental, the teacher should prepare some simple drills which clarify the problem.

| 6 | 7 | 1 | 7 | 6 | 5 | 6 |
| La | Ti | Do | Ti | La | Si | La |

Exercises in the *melodic minor scale* will provide experience with the altered sixth and seventh scale tones.

| 6 | 7 | 1 | 7 | 6 | 5 | 4 | 4 | 3 | 3 | 3 | 6 | 6 | 3 | 3 | 4 | 5 | 6 |
| La | Ti | Do | Ti | La | Sol | Fa | Fa | Mi | Mi | Mi | Sol | Sol | Mi | Mi | Fi | Si | La |

Once these exercises have been mastered, the class may turn in their books to minor key songs which involve a few chromatically altered notes. As with all the other aspects of the music-reading program, great care must be taken to see that growth in reading minor melodies is slow and steady. The children must feel secure in handling the new mode and the frequent chromatics. The teacher should always stress the importance of *understanding* the particular reading problem at hand. Rather than playing or singing a troublesome passage for the children, the wise teacher will guide the class in solving it themselves.

Reading music in three parts.   Most sixth-grade songbooks in the basic music series contain a few songs in three parts. Some of the songs are actually in two parts with an optional descant. Simple contrapuntal pieces will occasionally be found, and there will certainly be three-part chordal-style compositions with the melody predominantly in the top voice.

Because of the rather limited range of children's voices in the sixth grade, the lowest part in these three-part arrangements will often center around middle C. The problem of reading leger lines will therefore develop. The teacher should give some time to preparing simple exercises which will familiarize the students with notation in the following ranges:

| 1 | 5 | 6 | 7 | 1 | 2 | 1 | 7 | 7 | 7 | 6 | 6 | 5 |
| Do | Sol | La | Ti | Do | Re | Do | Ti | Ti | Ti | La | La | Sol |

Not all the students in the sixth grade are able to sing easily in this low range. At no time should these notes be sung loudly with a chest tone. However, many of the more physically mature boys will find music written in this range most appealing, for their voices have begun to change. These boys sing high notes only with considerable strain and embarrassment and are really much happier when singing their own comfortably arranged part.

The many problems of the boy's changing voice are traditionally reserved for the teacher in junior high school. However, more attention could be given these problems in the sixth grade; learning to read music fluently in this range

will be most helpful to those students whose voices will soon be much deeper. In fact, a school system which conscientiously carries out the program of music-reading studies presented here will find that the junior high school music program will be extraordinarily successful. Students entering the seventh grade will understand the rudiments of notation and its translation into sound. They will be familiar with the keyboard and they will be able to express themselves intelligently with regard to letter names and time values of notes, as well as tempo, dynamics, and other items of musical expression. Students in possession of this knowledge will be ready for music instruction of a considerably higher level than that commonly encountered in junior high school music classes.

CONCLUSION

The music-reading activities presented here should be but a part of the elementary school music program; the ability to read music notation is only one way that a child may learn to love and understand the art of music. Listening to music, learning beautiful songs by rote, and participating in joyful rhythmic activities are all of great importance during the early years of music study. Yet, the ability to read music permits one to study the literature of music without the presence of a teacher; learning may thus continue long after the more transitory experiences of elementary school have terminated. It is to this period of growth that this book is dedicated.

SUGGESTIONS FOR FURTHER STUDY

GARRETSON, Robert L. *Music in Childhood Education*. New York: Appleton-Century-Crofts, 1966. Pages 205–225.

RUNKLE, Aleta, and ERICKSEN, Mary LeBow. *Music for Today's Boys and Girls*. Boston: Allyn and Bacon, 1966. Pages 162–164, 200–201, 222–236, 269–272.

SWANSON, Bessie. *Music in the Education of Children*, 2nd ed. Belmont, Cal.: Wadsworth, 1964. Pages 172–184.

Appendix A

The Music-Reading Continuum

IN PRESENTING this sequence of instructional steps, the author wishes to state that he is highly aware of the subjectivity involved in devising such a pattern of learning. The music-reading continuum presented here is simply a series of musical experiences arranged in a manner which may produce an understanding of music notation and some ability in translating music symbols into sound.

Hopefully, this continuum will assist the inexperienced teacher in organizing his elementary music classes and in keeping them moving toward the goal of ability in reading music. The older teacher may use it to check the sequence of activities in each grade and to determine the degree of advancement of his students. Regular review of previously mastered steps should be an important part of all music classes progressing on the continuum.

The numbers in parentheses following each step indicate the page in this book where the particular item is discussed.

1. Becoming aware of the art of music (10)
2. Being exposed to the performance of beautiful music (12)
3. Experimenting with sounds. (11)
4. Developing an interest in listening to music. (10)
5. Actively participating in the performance of music. (11)
6. Attempting to sing two notes of small intervals and short phrases of melody. (11)
7. Matching tones sung by the parent, teacher, or another child. (11)
8. Matching tones played on the bells or other fixed pitch instruments. (12)
9. Learning simple songs by rote. (12)
10. Learning to play simple instruments by rote. (12)
11. Discovering repetition in music (aural). (16, 22)
12. Accompanying songs on rhythm instruments. (12)
13. Learning songs with simple actions. (17, 18)
14. Playing bells and other fixed pitch instruments. (12)
15. Playing the autoharp. (12)
16. Developing a spirit of creativity. (13)
17. Improvising texts to tone-calls and phrases of melody. (13)
18. Creating additional verses to songs. (13)
19. Composing new melodies for the class to sing. (13)
20. Developing discriminating listening habits. (12, 13)
21. Responding to walking, running, and skipping music with the appropriate movement. (14)
22. Substituting spoken words for walking, running, and skipping music. (14)
23. Playing walking, running, and skipping music on a drum other instrument. (14)
24. Doing the three previous activities simultaneously (14, 15)
25. Pantomiming familiar songs while the music is played. (18)
26. Recognizing when musical tones move *up* or *down*. (41)
27. Expressing *up* and *down* with the hand while listening to instruments or voices. (41)

28. Choosing the correct chord while accompanying singing on the autoharp. (12)
29. Developing expression in rote singing. (59, 60)
30. Becoming aware of different tempos and moods in music. (12, 59)
31. Discovering loud and soft, fast and slow, *crescendo* and *diminuendo*. (59, 60)
32. Developing a feeling for beat, an awareness of tempo, and a sense of meter. (25)
33. Learning simple traditional folk dances. (18-20)
34. Understanding the concept of musical phrases. (15, 16)
35. Responding to contrasting musical phrases with different movements through space. (16, 17)
36. Creating new movements to familiar folk-dance tunes. (18, 19)
37. Becoming acquainted with printed music notation and music books. (20-23)
38. Developing eye movement from left to right. (20, 26)
39. Watching the music while singing familiar songs. (20)
40. Discovering repetition in music symbols (visual). (22, 23)
41. Learning to recognize familiar tunes from observing the music. (21)
42. Attempting to sing new songs by observing the music while the teacher plays or sings. (21)
43. Reading quarter and eighth notes with the words *walk* and *run* respectively. (26)
44. Learning the legitimate music names for walking and running notes (quarter and eighth). (26)
45. Pointing along rows of quarter and eighth notes while the chants *walk* or *run*. (26)
46. Playing quarter and eighth notes on a drum or other rhythm instrument. (26)
47. Recognizing aurally quarter or eighth notes when played on a drum. (26)

48. Finding quarter and eighth notes in music books. (27)
49. Learning to write quarter and eighth notes. (27)
50. Expressing quarter and eighth notes in physical motion (walk and run). (27)
51. Chanting and playing simple rhythmic patterns comprised of quarter and eighth notes. (27, 28)
52. Writing patterns of quarter and eighth notes as dictated by the teacher. (28, 29)
53. Reading simple rhythmic accompaniments to familiar songs. (35, 36)
54. Singing from a five-tone scale ladder. (44, 45)
55. Singing familiar tunes with numbers. (46)
56. Composing simple, five-tone melodies with numbers. (46)
57. Singing new melodies written in numbers. (46)
58. Taking dictation with numbers. (46, 47)
59. Continuing to grow in musical experiences. (29, 30)
60. Experimenting with the metronome. (31, 32)
61. Learning about half notes, dotted half notes, whole notes, dotted eighth and sixteenth notes, and the quarter rest. (30, 31)
62. Learning the aural relationship of notes of different rhythmic values. (31, 32)
63. Becoming familiar with the staff. (48, 49)
64. Reading simple tonal patterns and melodies from the staff. (50, 51)
65. Playing number melodies on the bells or organ. (54, 55)
66. Developing a vocabulary of tonal patterns in E or E-flat major. (67)
67. Reading pitch and rhythm simultaneously in simple songs in E or E-flat major. (51, 52)
68. Reading rhythmic accompaniments to piano pieces. (37)
69. Playing compositions for rhythm instruments alone. (37)
70. Observing new music in print while the teacher plays or sings. (21)
71. Learning to sing from an extended scale ladder. (48)

72. Singing songs with descants and *ostanati.* (77)
73. Singing rounds and canons. (77)
74. Gaining experience in reading many simple songs in E-flat or E major. (51-54)
75. Learning the music symbols for loud and soft. (61)
76. Observing directions for dynamics while playing instruments. (60)
77. Taking dictation in dynamics. (61, 62)
78. Expressing two or more note values in physical motion simultaneously. (31, 32)
79. Studying dotted quarter and eighth notes. (32, 33)
80. Understanding beat, tempo, and meter. (25, 30, 31)
81. Learning about measures and measure signatures. (33)
82. Learning the conducting patterns. (34)
83. Moving to the key of F major. (68)
84. Reading tonal patterns in F major. (69)
85. Learning to read music with *one* on the first *space.* (68, 69)
86. Learning how to locate the keynote according to the key signature; reading in several major keys. (70-72)
87. Learning the letter names of the lines and spaces in the treble staff. (72, 73)
88. Understanding sharps, flats, and naturals. (73)
89. Learning to play any note, sharp or flat, on the keyboard. (73, 74)
90. Remembering the pitch of certain letters, such as A. (73)
91. Learning the symbols for accent, *crescendo,* and *diminuendo.* (62)
92. Improving one's ability to read by observation. (21, 53, 54, 75, 76)
93. Continuing to grow in one's ability to play the piano and organ. (72-74)
94. Harmonizing by ear. (79)
95. Reading simple exercises in two parts. (78, 79)
96. Being able to read either part in a two-part song. (77, 78)
97. Singing accidentals. (74, 75)

98. Recognizing melodies written in the minor mode. (82)
99. Using *six* as the home tone when reading in minor. (82)
100. Reading complete songs in minor keys. (83-85)
101. Reading three-part music. (85)
102. Using an eighth note as the beat note. (79, 80)
103. Learning to conduct slow $\frac{6}{8}$ patterns. (80)
104. Learning to use the dotted quarter note as the beat note. (81)
105. Conducting fast $\frac{6}{8}$ music. (81, 82)
106. Reading fluently in the leger lines below the treble staff. (85, 86)
107. Reading music at sight, without the aid of numbers, syllables, the piano, or a teacher. (86)

Appendix B   Music-Reading Activities By Grade Level

WHEN ORGANIZING his classes, the music teacher should be guided largely by the continuum as a whole, rather than by this grade-by-grade sequence, for growth in music reading is the result of logical, organized musical experiences. The following outline of activities arranged by grade may be helpful in developing an elementary music course of study with emphasis in music reading. The suggested steps in the continuum to be accomplished at each grade level are, of course, merely indications of work which might be accomplished at that level and may not be attainable in some situations.

Kindergarten–Grade One: Continuum steps 1 through 25. Emphasis upon exposure to fine music, stimulation of interest in active participation and experimentation, nourishment of the child's inherent creative spirit. De-emphasis on specific, technical accomplishments.

Grade Two: Review, continuation, and expansion of activities in grade one. Continuum steps through about number 58. Much concentration on developing strong sense of beat. Emphasis on physical expression of rhythm. Improvement of pitch-deficient children. Development of acuity of hearing. In general, more attention to rhythmic aspects of music than to pitch, but some pitch reading with numbers should be started.

Grade Three: Regular review of previous musical experiences. Study of continuum steps through number 74. Much attention to development of pitch sense. Emphasis upon studying the printed page of music. Much growth in singing ability (rounds, descants, etc.).

Grade Four: Careful scrutiny of the early steps of the continuum to avoid continuing study built on weak foundations. Continuum steps through about 91. Much work on technical accomplishments. Reading many melodies in several keys. Renewed emphasis on instruments, especially keyboard.

Grade Five: Continuum steps through number 97. Continued growth in vocal ability—part singing and reading accidentals. Much emphasis in observation reading. Increasing ability at the keyboard.

Grade Six: Completion of the continuum with mastery of reading in minor and understanding compound rhythms. Secure understanding of the technical aspects of music notation. A growing awareness of our vast heritage of music.

Bibliography

ANDREWS, Gladys. *Creative Rhythmic Movement for Children.* Englewood Cliffs, N. J.: Prentice-Hall, 1954.

CARABO-CONE, Madeleine. *The Playground as Music Teacher.* New York: Harper & Brothers, 1959.

DOLL, Edna, and NELSON, Mary Jarman. *Rhythms Today!* Morristown, N. J.: Silver Burdette, 1965.

ELLISON, Alfred. *Music with Children.* New York: McGraw-Hill, 1959.

GARRETSON, ROBERT L. *Music in Childhood Education.* New York: Appleton-Century-Crofts, 1966.

HOLZ, Emil A., and JACOBI, Roger E. *Teaching Band Instruments to Beginners.* Englewood Cliffs, N. J.: Prentice-Hall, 1966.

HOOD, Marguerite V., and SCHULTZ, E. J. *Learning Music Through Rhythm.* Boston: Ginn, 1949.

KODALY, Zoltan. *Let Us Sing Correctly.* London: Boosey and Hawkes, 1952.

McMILLAN, L. Eileen. *Guiding Children's Growth Through Music.* Boston: Ginn, 1959.

NORDHOLM, Harriet. *Singing in the Elementary Schools.* Englewood Cliffs, N. J.: Prentice-Hall, 1966.

NYE, Robert E., and BERGETHON, Bjornar. *Basic Music for Classroom Teachers,* 2nd ed. Englewood Cliffs, N. J.: Prentice-Hall, 1962.

NYE, Robert E., and NYE, Vernice T. *Music in the Elementary School,* 2nd ed. Englewood Cliffs, N. J.: Prentice-Hall, 1964.

RUNKLE, Aleta, and ERICKSEN, Mary LeBow. *Music for Today's Boys and Girls.* Boston: Allyn and Bacon, 1966.

SHEEHY, Emma D. *Children Discover Music and Dance.* New York: Holt, Rinehart and Winston, 1959.

SWANSON, Bessie. *Music in the Education of Children,* 2nd ed. Belmont, Cal.: Wadsworth, 1964.

TIMMERMAN, Maurine. *Let's Teach Music in the Elementary School.* Evanston, Ill.: Summy-Birchard, 1958.